RITA

SAINT OF
THE IMPOSSIBLE

by Jo Lemoine

translated by
Sr. Florestine Audette, RJM

St. Paul Books & Media

Library of Congress Cataloging-in-Publication Data

Lemoine, Jo.
  [Rita, la sainte des impossibles. English]
  Rita, saint of the impossibles / Jo Lemoine ; translated by Sr.
Florestine Audette.
      p.   cm.
  ISBN 0-8198-6422-6
  1. Rita, of Cascia, Saint, 1381?-1457. 2. Christian saints-
Italy—Biography.   I. Title.
BX4700.R5L4513   1992
282'.092—dc20   92-34919
[B]   CIP

Cover illustration by Christopher J. Pelicano

Original title: *Rita: la sainte des impossibiles*
Copyright © Mediaspaul, 8 rue Madame, 75006 Paris
Translated from the French by Sr. Florestine Audette, RJM

English edition copyright © 1992, Daughters of St. Paul

Printed and published in the U.S.A. by St. Paul Books & Media, 50 St. Paul's
Avenue, Boston, MA 02130.

St. Paul Books & Media is the publishing house of the Daughters of St. Paul, an
international congregation of women religious serving the Church with the
communications media.

        1 2 3 4 5 6 7 8 9   99 98 97 96 95 94 93 92

Contents

Foreword

What does a fifteenth-century saint have to say to the person on his or her journey in the twentieth century? Rita of Cascia was a wife, a mother and a religious. The events of her life were like the links in a chain that led her to Jesus.

Rita was a youthful, charming bride who walked down the aisle of her parish church to be joined in marriage to a man she had not chosen—Paul de Ferdinand. She was the only child of a devout, now elderly couple, and her marriage had been arranged by a father who wanted his daughter to be secure and settled in a nearby cottage. Rita's plea to become a religious had been overruled. Through all of her tears, she realized that the Lord was asking her to find her Savior in the image of a husband whose handsome face did not conceal the violence of his temper.

The bruises which soon appeared on Rita's face and arms told a story without words. Rita prayed, fasted and begged the Lord for her husband's conversion. She never complained to others about him. She who loved to meditate the passion of Christ learned to walk with Jesus on the Calvary road of her married life. She remained true to Paul and silently won him to the Lord. The lion gradually became kind, compassionate and loyal to his marital commitment. He became a loving father to the couple's twin boys. When Paul was murdered, his widow wept and forgave his assassin. Her adolescent sons sought revenge; Rita prayed and did penance for them. They both became seriously ill and died in the spirit of Christian forgiveness. Humanly speaking, Rita was now all alone. But there was One who had been even more alone when his apostles had run away. The widow would find solace and comfort in the Lord.

Through divine intervention, she was able to realize her dream of becoming an Augustinian nun.

Sister Rita spent herself in works of kindness for her community and the poor of Cascia who came to the monastery door.

She received a thorn—like the thorns which encircled the Master's head—embedded in her brow. This thorn festered into a frightful, evil-smelling wound. Few could stay near Rita and the isolation she found in her little cell was melted by the love she felt for Jesus and her desire to be with him in his agony in the garden. She wanted to be among the small band of sisters who would go on pilgrimage to Rome for the Holy Year of 1450. Her wound healed before the journey began and re-opened after she returned home. She witnessed the canonization of St. Bernardine of Siena. If only she could have known that 550 years later on May 24, 1900, Pope Leo XIII would canonize her!

The documented miracles that took place happened during St. Rita's life and also in the years since her death are signs of the Lord's pleasure with her. Yet, the greatest gift that Rita leaves to people of every age is the secret ancient and new: saints are made by doing God's will with love until death.

Sr. Susan Helen Wallace, FSP

Chapter 1

A Long-Awaited Child

Tap, tap, tap! Tap, tap, tap!

From the steep heights overlooking the narrow valley rose rhythmic echoes of a wooden paddle beating wet linen. On the edge of a mountain stream, a woman, already mature in age, shivered as she drew a woolen shawl around her shoulders. It was cool here in the mountains on this October evening.

The year was 1380; the setting, Rocca-Porena, a tiny mountain village near the city of Cascia in Umbria. In the future, this autonomous region would be joined to other small peninsular states to form the country of Italy. But that would happen much later. Right now, these unruly principalities were tearing each other to pieces and rebelling against the Pope and the civil leaders who wanted to annex them.

It had been only three years since the exiled Pope had left Avignon and occupied the Holy See. Gregory XI had come back to Rome only to die there. And his successor, Urban VI, was now hard put to defend the Church against the threats of mutually destructive divisions and heresies.

Amata was unaware of these things. All she knew was that these were troubled times. It was not good for her to linger alone beyond the village limits after sunset. And so, she was now losing no time in rinsing the family laundry, heedless of the cold water chapping her hands. Already, the sun was sinking behind the nearby mountaintops, leaving a few golden rays scattered in the sky. The gray of evening would soon settle, as gray was gradually settling in the washerwoman's hair. Had time flown by so quickly since the day of her marriage to Antonio Lotti? On this doleful evening, Amata had a keener sense of the aching sorrow deep in her heart. No, she would never have them, those children for whom they had both been praying for more than twelve years.

But there was Antonio, her Antonio. Coming back from the forest where he had worked all day, he was here to fetch his wife. He, too, had a few touches of gray sprinkled in his black head of hair. His pace had lost some of its former vitality. But he was still strong and, without a word, he picked up the heavy bundle of clothes. This considerate attitude was quite unusual in the countryside of these times. It would bring the neighboring women, lingering on their doorsteps, to say, as the couple entered the village, "Those two really love each other. What a pity that heaven doesn't answer their plea and bless their marriage. They want a child so much."

But was it really too late?

A few weeks had gone by. In the house, Amata was preparing pasta for the evening meal. She felt tired and gave a start when she heard two loud knocks at the door. Happily, she was not alone. Antonio was near the fireplace, repairing a kitchen utensil. When he opened the door, he found himself face to face with two villagers he knew very well: Lucio and Pietro.

Their faces were contorted with rage. Nevertheless, they greeted Antonio politely as they tried to regain some of their composure. They had nothing against the Lottis. On the contrary, they were coming to ask the couple to act as referees in their quarrel. People of Rocca-Porena often had this kind of recourse to the Lottis, whom they silently regarded as peace-makers.

When asked to be seated and explain themselves, both of them broke out in mounting tones of anger.

"If I find your wild hens in my vegetables again, I'll shoot them!" shouted Lucio.

"Look now, you just have to mend your fence!" Pietro quickly retorted. "As for killing my chickens, I'd like to see you do that. You'd be the first one dead, because I...."

Amata kept away from the group and resumed her domestic duties. But from this distance, she looked over at her husband. Antonio knew very well that, while he was searching for arguments good enough to calm down two antagonists, she was supporting him with her prayers. This question of joint use of the vegetable patch was an excuse to revive a much deeper and older feud. The two men belonged to families who had fought on opposing sides in the past. The least incident was enough to fan the smoldering flames of hatred.

No, these two antagonists would not come to blows. Once again, Antonio managed to find the necessary words, to reason with the one, to calm the other, to promise to help them mend the fence. He had not learned this from books, which neither he nor his wife could read. He had learned this solely from the book of life. Experience, love of peace and, above all, love of God: these had taught him how to conduct his life and radiate serenity into the lives of others.

In those still-primitive days, faith was taught in churches by words and images. Paintings and pictures helped the faithful to become familiar with the childhood and passion of Christ and with the stories of saints who had tried to walk in his footsteps. Amata and Antonio now wished to follow this path marked out by their forefathers. That was the sum of their knowledge. But it was adequate to meet their needs.

Antonio was worried. His wife had been pale and trembling all evening. She had hardly eaten anything. The following day she was depressed. This was unusual for Amata, who had never been emotional to the point of being disturbed by a quarrel that was of no concern to her. Besides, peace had been restored between their neighbors. So, what was the difficulty?

The following week, Antonio learned the truth. Returning home at an unusual time of the day, he found his wife in deep conversation with the *Mamma*, a good old lady of the area who gave motherly care and advice to everyone in the neighborhood. When the couple were alone again, Amata, her eyes radiant with happiness, led him to the statue of the Blessed Mother, exclaiming, "Antonio, let's give thanks! You know...the baby! I am certain now! God is good!"

The baby? Rapt in thought, Amata had often had the child on her mind during the last few months as she strolled along the edge of the mountain stream where spring was timidly blossoming again. She did not come here anymore to do her laundry. She was preparing herself for the long-awaited birth, and she had to take a few precautions because she was not young anymore. But she walked every day amid this untamed and awe-inspiring nature which she loved so much. Her child would be imbued with beauty. God's creation was so beautiful. Rejuvenated, as it were, the sun caressed the windswept summits. The breeze, soft and light, was already speaking of beautiful days to come.

In a few weeks, the child would be there. The expectant mother had prepared for its coming. Everything was tidy in the little house of Rocca-Porena, ready to welcome the baby. But she had not told the Mamma what she and her husband were still the only ones to know: the child would be a little girl. Amata was sure.

Her conviction had not come from a simple intuition, such as women in her condition sometimes have, or from mistaking her wishes or dreams for reality. This certitude had come from on high.

It had happened at the very dawn of the great hope. A bright sun had shed a golden light over the garden that mild autumn day. Amata had taken advantage of the fine weather to carry out a few seasonal tasks. As she cast her eye on some denuded clumps, she could recall the sight of them once covered with her favorite flowers, especially with roses. That had been but a short time ago. And it would happen again when the round of seasons would bring summer to Rocca-Porena. But, by that time, the child would have been born and would sleep in the shade of the old cypress tree.

This thought rejoiced the heart of the expectant mother. Once more, she silently thanked the Lord for this long awaited joy, she tried not to feel apprehensive. Everything would be fine. And Antonio would be happy to have a son.

At that moment, there had come a gust of wind and the murmur of a voice. "Do not fear, Amata," she heard. "You will give birth not to a boy but girl. But you and Antonio will love her very much. And the Lord will love her still more!"

That evening, after some hesitation, she had confided to

Antonio the words of the angel, for this could come from no one but an angel, could it? Taken by surprise and awed with respect, her husband had immediately asserted that he would whole-heartedly greet and welcome this little rose into their home. How well they should try to bring up this little child in whom God was already showing interest!

And now in the springtime—just a few moments ago, on this very spot near the edge of the water, Amata had again heard the voice from heaven saying, "Amata, the day is drawing near. You will name this child Rita, in honor of St. Margherita. Through her, this little name will become a great name."

Amata felt still more awestruck than before. A similar apparition had been mentioned in the Gospel: the annunciation of the Messiah's birth. There had also been the announcement that Elizabeth, the elderly woman who had no more hopes of having a child, would be a mother. The Lord had had special plans for the child that Elizabeth and Zechariah named John.

What destiny could the little peasant girl of Umbria have in common with the precursor of the Messiah, the fearless John the Baptist? Amata shivered with excitement and hurried home to tell Antonio about this new intervention from heaven. Why was God taking such an interest in their child?

━━━━━━━━━━

It was May, 1381. In the Lotti home, a little girl had just been born. Happiness had entered the house along with her. As Antonio proudly presented his daughter to the visitors, he seemed to not even remember that he had once hoped for a son. She was pretty, this little Rita, with her dark eyes, her already abundant brown hair and her milk-white complexion. In her large bed, Amata, overwhelmed with joy, was turning her grateful thoughts to God.

But the name was puzzling everyone. Why had they chosen St. Margherita as the child's patron? This was a tradition of neither the Lottis nor the Mancinis—Amata's own family. And what a strange idea to have given the girl this shortened form of the saint's name when she was baptized at St. Mary's Church at Cascia.

The parents kept their lips sealed on their secret. For them, this name symbolized what their child should become: Margherita meant a *pearl*. It also meant a *flower* with a golden heart and white petals. Piety, purity, generosity—these were the virtues they hoped their daughter would possess. They would not merely hope she would have them, but they would try to help her acquire them.

For a time, Rita was just a baby girl easy to attend to. She seldom cried and she quickly learned to recognize her father and mother. Very soon she began to smile at them. When they went to work in the fields or the forest, they would bring her along in a wicker basket and leave her sleeping in the shade not far from wherever they were working.

One sunny day, Antonio and Amata were busy in a good-sized field. They were at the far end of a furrow. Near the road, on the embankment, lay little Rita in her usual plain crib. She appeared to be asleep. But at times her eyes would open and her little hands would gently move about.

A reaper hurried by. He had just cut himself with his scythe while working in the neighboring field and was striding along back to the village to nurse a large, bleeding gash on his right hand.

All of a sudden, he heard a soft buzzing. He stopped and discovered the baby, surrounded by a swarm of bees. His instinctive move was to ignore his wound and try to chase the insects away. But nothing could stop them. The bees kept circling around Rita's face. Some even entered her mouth and came out again, as if they were playing at the entrance of their hive.

The astounding fact was that the baby did not cry or scream. Wide awake by now, little Rita followed with her eyes the unceasing dance of the bees, which would neither touch her, nor sting her, nor do her any harm.

The amazed harvester had now stopped waving his hand, since his help was not needed. Suddenly, he could not remember which of his hands had been injured. Both were perfectly smooth and healthy. It was as if his efforts to protect Rita had drawn a miraculous healing upon himself.

He quickly went to relate his experience to Rita's parents. Then, in spite of their recommendations, he repeated his story throughout the village.

Why had this little daughter of Antonio and Amata Lotti, this child only a few months old, been favored with such protection from heaven? Yet her future seemed destined to unfold, uneventful and commonplace, in the hamlet of Rocca-Porena. Such were the comments made by women lingering in the warm village lanes while the sun was slowly sinking below the horizon.

Chapter 2

Child of the Mountain

Season followed upon season—scorching summers, dreary autumns, winters more or less severe, blossoming springs. The little girl was now four years old.

She was lively and gracious, this child whom Antonio and Amata Lotti had wanted for so long. Even now, they could hardly believe that this happiness was really theirs. Every morning brought them the same breathless wonder as they hugged their daughter, waking from her sleep. They could hardly remember the times when their home had felt so lifeless in spite of their mutual love. It seemed to them that many years had passed since then.

First, Rita began smiling at her parents as she prattled along. Then, she went through the vague motions of her first kisses, uttered her first words, took her first steps. Amata would bring Rita's little hands together and teach her to mumble a prayer and make the sign of the cross. The little girl, awakening to life, was becoming acquainted with her parents and with Christ, the Virgin Mary and the saints. She embraced them all with the same love.

Like all mothers, Amata wanted to dress her little girl in pretty clothes on feastdays. One of those peddlers who scoured mountains and plains came to offer the inhabitants of those remote areas a few pieces of fabric, some cheap lace and especially ribbons. Ribbons of all colors would deck one's hair so prettily. Several mothers had bought some of these for their little girls, because it was now the season for outdoor festivities. On the following Sunday, there would be a Corpus Christi procession in Cascia. Each mother wanted her child to look her best to accompany Jesus with bouquets of roses.

"Rita! Come and see...."

From the peddler's display, Amata had chosen a few white and pink ribbons. Which would suit her daughter's complexion and curls? She wanted to try them out and compare.

But, pffft...! No more Rita. She had taken flight to the far end of the garden. A mischievous smile and a wave of her hand clearly indicated, "No! No!"

Somewhat annoyed, Amata put the frippery back in place and apologized to the peddler. He, not too happy about the whole affair, packed his merchandise and set off again up the steep-sloped path at the slow pace of his mule. He grumbled about the sale which had come to nothing, thanks to that "little brat."

Some time later, when Rita was asked why she had refused the ribbons, she found herself at a loss. Then, with her irresistible smile, she said, "Jesus will love me just as much without the ribbons. He knows that I love him so much." She had already understood that beauty of soul is the only beauty that matters.

A few more summers and winters had passed. Rita was nearly nine years old. The strength and nimbleness that she was developing with the years, her parents, on the contrary, were gradually losing. In order that she might grow, they had to diminish. This is the law of nature. It is especially true of children who come late in the lives of their parents.

Mrs. Lotti did not have to ask her daughter to help with the household duties. Without being told to do so, Rita assumed her share, gradually increasing it as she grew older.

"Let me go to the well, Mamma. I can carry the water jug by myself now."

"Daddy, take me into the forest with you. I'll help you tie up the bundles of firewood and bring them back."

When her parents protested, Rita would invariably reply, "I'm strong, you know that!"

Yes, she was strong of body and soul, this Rita Lotti. Companionship with adults, and with adults advanced in years, had matured her mind quickly. Of course, she loved to sing and laugh. But more and more, she assumed responsibilities. She watched over her parents' health and the general running of the home. Antonio and Amata developed the habit of consulting her when decisions and arrangements had to be made, even for comforting and counseling neighbors and friends.

Now, Rita was the one who did the laundry at the edge of the mountain stream. Kneeling at the very spot where her mother had labored, it was her turn to admire the high mountains. She knew that along these mountain trails could still be found traces of ancient hermitages very high up in practically inaccessible nooks. Holy people had lived there in the past, totally taken up with the glory of God and the salvation of the people of their time.

At twelve, at fourteen, Rita was growing in faith. Her Christian belief was becoming personal and reasoned. She wished she could devote herself to the contemplation of Jesus on the cross, could unite her sufferings to those of her Savior. Her youth and filial duties prevented her from doing this. But she at least managed to isolate herself now and then right in the family home to pray. Her parents, who understood her wish, allowed her to set aside a little area in the house for her own specific use. There, she would pray to the Blessed Virgin and to John the Baptist, one of her favorite saints. There, especially, she would meditate on the passion of our Lord.

Like everyone else in these valleys, Rita had heard people speak about St. Francis of Assisi. He had sown the seeds of charity in his footsteps during the previous century. Like him, she wanted to prove her love for Jesus by doing good around her. No matter how little she had, she would wholeheartedly share it. The unfortunate knew her very well. Rita did not hesitate to seek them out, even along the rough mountain paths. And as she denied herself to bring them some material comforts, she also comforted them with her smile, her kind words, and her willingness to listen to their complaints.

Like all adolescents of all times, she would dream of her future. But for her the future was seen as a life totally given to God and to others. Religious life.... This was her dream but she was still young. It was a matter of waiting a while yet. She dreaded the thought of hurting her aging parents, but she trusted that Providence would help her when it would be time to tell them about her secret wish.

Meanwhile, Rita's parents were concerned about their daughter's future. Feeling that they would soon leave this world, they did not want to leave her all alone. Moreover, until their departure they needed her so very, very much. They needed her care, her help, her cheerfulness, her love.

One day, as Rita was returning from a visit to a poor woman living at the edge of the forest, she saw a young man, well dressed and of proud bearing, coming out of her home. Antonio was at the door, seeing him out with deep bows of respect. When his daughter drew near, he motioned her to follow him inside.

Somewhat surprised, but not giving the matter much thought, the girl entered the house and put down her basket. Her mother's gesture gave her to understand that the preparation of the meal was to be put off, and that she must first listen to her father.

He began in a tone somewhat more solemn than usual. "I have just had a visit from Paul de Ferdinand. We have already met several times since he has returned to our country. I have sold him some fodder in the past. He is an excellent horseman and owns at least two horses."

Rita said nothing. She thought there was no need to respond. Antonio went on and Amata now put in her word. As many elderly people like to do, the Lottis recalled the childhood and youth of the young man in question and his degrees of kinship with this one and that one.

Of course, the Lotti couple were charitable people and did not like to speak ill of their fellow human beings. Therefore, they did not dwell on the objectionable aspects of Paul's personality or behavior. But Rita had heard about him at Rocca-Porena, where he was feared but little loved. Everyone knew that he had been active in the recent war and that he was still in touch with the leaders of one of the factions. The region had barely begun to calm down. There were still strife and quarrels, in which Paul loved to become involved.

He was a handsome man, this Paul de Ferdinand—tall, dark, strong and bold. No one could deny that he was brave. But he sometimes went so far as to be brutal. Moreover, he was a drunkard and a pleasure-seeker. Rita recalled hearing that, a few evenings before, Paul had again caused a commotion at the Four Roads' Inn just because the waiters had taken too long to bring him a jug of Asti wine.

The girl turned her thoughts away from this subject, which did not inspire her in the least. She judged it should now be time to pour the soup over the bread, but she dared not rise from her chair. Something her father had just said brought her back to reality.

"Paul de Ferdinand is preparing for marriage," Antonio had said. "He will definitely settle here and he has already chosen his future wife."

"The poor girl!" Rita thought to herself.

She felt sorry for whomever would be afflicted with such a husband. As for herself, she had consecrated her life to the Lord some time before. She was waiting until she would be a little older to ask Antonio's permission to enter a convent. Marriage matters were of no interest to her.

Suddenly, she started. No! This could not be true! As she was distractedly listening to Antonio, she suddenly grasped the fact that the "poor girl" was to be herself, Rita Lotti! Paul de Ferdinand had come to ask for her hand in marriage.

Rita protested. She confided to her parents her promise to enter religious life and her irrevocable intention of keeping that promise. She had no right to marry.

It was a waste of time and energy. She was made to understand that, on the contrary, she'd had no right to make this vow validly without her father's authorization. And Antonio Lotti was far from approving this "rash" commitment. He wanted to marry his daughter to Paul and he would do it.

In a gentler manner, Amata explained to the girl that, according to her own experience, marriage was not an obstacle to prayer. Rita would be able to pray in her home as well as anywhere else. This state of life, sanctified by a sacrament, would surely allow her to work out her salvation. Rita cried, prayed, cried some more and prayed some more. Her parents, on the one hand, and her Father in heaven, on the other, seemed to remain insensitive to her pleas.

We must not believe that Antonio and Amata did not love their daughter, nor that they did not love the Lord. They simply perceived matters from a human perspective. As they were getting on in years, they dreaded leaving Rita behind without any protection. Times were uncertain. Married to Paul de Ferdinand, Rita would be assured of her keep and would have someone to defend her should the need arise.

Another advantage was that she would be near them, living in a village house close by. They would be able to see her every day. She would help them, nursing them till they would breathe their last.

The suitor's social rank, slightly above their own, was also bound to impress Rita's parents a little. Still more, there was his bad-temper. Paul was violent and spiteful. It would be better for the Lottis to be among his friends than his enemies. If he were to be refused the girl he had singled out from afar, he would create a scandal throughout the neighborhood. Amata dreaded the possibility of violence.

This was a promising situation her parents thought. Poor Rita!

Days went by. Rita saw the doors of heaven close before her, as it were. She did not lose faith—not that! But time was working against her. With each meeting with Paul her hopes dwindled. She had had to agree to see her fiancé, since Antonio had given his consent to their marriage. To welcome Paul in a worthy manner, not only did Rita have to make the house look beautiful and spend long hours in the kitchen, but, over and above that, she had to dress up to honor Paul when he visited. Where were the times when she had refused the ribbons Amata had offered her?

In keeping with local custom, her fiancé had loaves of bread, small pieces of jewelry and belts delivered to her, first by three women, then by three men. She had to accept these gifts and wear the jewelry and belts when Paul came to see her.

At least, was he pleasant with her? He was, insofar as his

violent temper and overbearing attitude allowed him to be so. But the least of his remarks revealed a domineering spirit, surely natural in a man of that time, but, more pronounced in him than in others: "When we're married, we'll do this. You'll do that. I don't want...."

And people were saying that he had not given up going to taverns or seeing girls "of loose morals," who were found in those places.

Why couldn't Rita free herself from this situation? At night she sobbed in the peaceful alcove that she would soon have to leave.

But, little by little, the young woman began to ask herself whether the total sacrifice to which she had aspired for such a long time—that is, to share in the passion of Christ—was not meant to take this strange form rather than what she had anticipated. On the other hand, the religious vocation had seemed sure, firm, urgent. How strange all this was!

Rita did not yet know that God sometimes traces straight paths with crooked lines.

Chapter 3

Woman Without a Grudge

The day of the wedding finally came. Unwittingly charming in her wedding attire, Rita solemnly pronounced the "yes" that would bind her future.

For this ceremony which, according to tradition, took place before twenty official witnesses chosen by the bridegroom—ten men and ten women—Paul de Ferdinand wished to appear at his best. His apparel and bearing justified the praise of his followers, who exclaimed, "What a proud lion!" He even made efforts to be amiable to his young wife, who could not help but anxiously ask herself, "Will this last?"

After the exchange of rings and the nuptial blessing, a first wedding banquet was held at the bridegroom's home. The only guests were his relatives and friends. This was the custom. The following week, a second banquet would gather the family and friends of the bride at the Lotti home. At first glance, this custom, which avoided the mingling of the two social sets, appeared to be far from neighborly. But undoubtedly this ruled out the likelihood of disputes about matters of precedence or of sharing the cost.

After all the rites had been performed, the couple were able to begin their life together. What would it be like?

———————————

Paul soon went back to his bad habits. Marriage had changed nothing in this respect. He began to be absent more and more frequently, to come home later and later at night. Often his torn clothes proved he had been in a fight, and he was obviously drunk. Poor Rita would patiently wait for him and, not allowing herself to make any comments, would heat up some food and mend the rents in Paul's clothes. In return, the excellent young housekeeper would receive only unkind remarks. "This cloak is poorly taken care of. Too much salt in this pie. See that you polish my hunting boots more carefully!"

One day, the master of the house was disturbed about a certain herb soup which, to his way of thinking, appeared on the menu too often. "Here's what I'm doing with it!"

The earthenware soup tureen fell in pieces at Rita's feet; she had barely had time to move back.

The following day, inquisitive neighbor women came for the news—while the fiery-tempered husband was away, of course.

"Whatever happened last night?"

"Paul had been drinking again, hadn't he?"

"My poor girl, if I had such a husband, I'd give him a piece of my mind!"

"It's nothing," Rita quietly replied. "He was only...a little nervous."

As they remembered the commotion they had heard, the gossips were not fooled. Yet, they could not help but silently admire the dignity of her whom they had nicknamed "*the woman without a grudge.*" More than one of them, in the wake of Rita's example, would try to be gentle and patient in her own home.

On the other hand, Paul de Ferdinand did have his better side. Sometimes he even showed himself generous—when he was in good spirits, or when good fortune had smiled upon him, or when a beggar crossed his path. He also knew how to help his friends when they were in need. But how difficult he was to live with! Nothing was ever to his liking. Now, in his outbursts of rage, he would go so far as to strike Rita.

Antonio and Amata would receive their daughter's visit every day. They could easily notice her reddened eyes and bruised arms, in spite of the efforts she made to hide them from her parents. When they would try to probe her with questions, she would answer evasively, "Why no, Father. Everything's all right."

"Why yes, Mamma, my health is good. I'm just tired."

They were advanced in years and she did not want them to worry. But the neighbor women were not so discreet. And so the elderly parents were beginning to ask themselves whether they had paved the way to a life of unhappiness for their "little girl."

Meanwhile, Rita continued to comfort and help the people in the village when she was aware they were in trouble or in financial difficulties. Her means now allowed her to be a little more generous materially than she had been in the past. But she gave much more by denying herself. She especially gave her time and her sympathetic attention. In a word, she gave her heart.

Since the day of her betrothal, she had also taken on a project, as bold as it was generous, to bring Paul back to better attitudes, to more sensible behavior and to the faith of his childhood.

"What a stupid idea," her relatives would undoubtedly have exclaimed had they known Rita's secret thoughts. So she was careful not to speak of this, even to her parents or to her childhood friends. God was the only one to whom she would confide this initiative, while she supported her prayers with many hidden sacrifices. Paul was often away; this made things easier for her. When he was home, he would not, or pretended he did not, notice the dark circles under his wife's eyes or how thin her face had become as a result of her privations. He would eat in haste, always in a hurry to leave again. Rita would wait on him and would take her "meal" later. In fact, she hardly ate at all, made three "Lents" of fasting a year instead of only one, and did other penances.

All the while, she continued to be graciously lovable, decking herself out as a woman of her status was expected to do. It was in line with the Gospel: "When you fast, anoint yourself and put on a happy expression so that your fasting is not obvious" (cf Mt 6:17).

As she silently offered her self-denial to her Father in heaven, Rita entrusted to him the same intention which had been dear to another sorrowful Christian woman of long ago, Monica the African mother. That intention was the conversion of her husband. Monica's husband had been a pagan, as well as a source of grief in the home. Yet, St. Augustine's mother had obtained the requested favor. Why should not the same be granted to this young Umbrian woman?

"So, Rita, when is the baby due?"

"Another two months to wait."

"Perhaps Paul's attitude will mellow when the baby is here."

The young woman did not respond to her neighbor's comment. Burdened with the child she was carrying, wearied by the self-denial that she continued to impose on herself, she kept her uncertainty hidden. The summer breeze was playing with the loose blades of grass along the mountain path she was now following. Rocky summits were etched against the blue sky. It felt good to be alive this morning.

"That may be true," Rita was thinking. For some time, Paul had been less violent. When he felt his anger rising, he would go for a walk out in the open and would come back appeased. He was especially hoping for a son.

Rita was unaware that, in spite of himself, her husband had finally been moved by her gentleness and by her steadfastness in fulfilling her duty. The woman who but a short time before had been chosen solely for her youthful charm, now appeared to him in her true worth, that of her spirit. And the prospect of fatherhood had confirmed these new attitudes in him. Rita simply noted the exterior changes and kept on praying.

Antonio and Amata Lotti would never experience the joy of knowing their grandchildren. In a short space of time, they both left this world for the heavenly reward promised in return for a long life of labor and generosity here on earth. However, they had had the opportunity to notice that their daughter seemed less anxious than at the beginning of her married life. Now from on high, they were undoubtedly helping her.

One fine morning, there was a great surprise! Two beautiful boys arrived in the de Ferdinand home. Paul's dreams of posterity were overwhelmingly fulfilled, as was Rita's motherly love.

The boys were baptized and respectively named James-Anthony and Paul-Marie. In this way, homage was rendered to the Blessed Virgin, to their father and to their grandfather.

With the arrival of the twins, peace settled upon the family for good. Paul de Ferdinand hardly ever had another fit of anger when something went against his wishes. Nor did he blame his wife for whatever had gone wrong.

As she watched her husband play with the twins, did Rita feel that she was understood and loved? Would she find a little happiness in the married life she had not chosen?

Disquieting signs first appeared one evening when Rita and the children were in the garden. Rita was coming and going, watering the flowers. She was followed by the small boys, who were beginning to walk and were not yet very firm on their feet.

"Don't come near. Watch out for the mud splashes!"

But it was fun, in spite of her warning, to run along the garden paths on their mother's heels.

"Rita! I can't find my leather belt!"

From the doorstep, Paul was calling his wife to help him, as husbands of all times have done to solve their clothing problems.

"Stay where you are, boys! I'll be back right away...."

The young mother hurriedly put down the half-filled bucket and rushed into the house.

Three minutes later, howls filled her heart with anxiety and brought her back to the garden. "Mamma! Mamma!" Paul-Marie was calling.

His brother had tried to lift the bucket and, naturally, had caused it to upset on the feet of both of them. Furious and soaking wet, they had come to blows and were pulling each other's hair at the same time. James-Anthony was the stronger of the two and his twin was crying for help.

With much difficulty, Rita managed to separate them and wipe them dry. At the same time, she tried to explain to them that they should never try to hurt one another. She sighed. Would the violence their father had painstakingly curbed reappear in her sons? Would they be able to overcome it as Paul had? How could she help them to do so?

Appeased and reconciled, they were once again laughing together, feeling good in their dry clothes. And Paul was laughing with them, exclaiming with amused pride, "What little lions!"

But Rita was worried.

This incident was to be repeated often during the boys' childhood. In spite of being very close, they loved to tease each other and to try their strength against one another, or against their friends. More serious was their tendency to harbor resentment against their rivals or opponents whenever the twins had not gotten the upper hand. This was a far cry from the Christian spirit Rita was trying to instill in them. Now she was dreaming of having a little girl, a gentle daughter whom she could fashion in her own image. Alas, that child would never come.

Tragedy was about to strike.

━━━━━━━━━━━

One winter evening, a storm was blowing with fury on Rocca-Porena. Supper had been waiting for a long time in the chimney-corner. In the candlelight, Rita, never idle, was spinning and praying. Some time before, the twins had returned from gathering sticks in the forest. They were chopping logs in the nearby shed. Almost adolescents now, they made themselves useful both inside and outside the house.

"Isn't Father home yet?" asked James-Anthony, as he came into the room.

"I'm hungry!" added Paul-Marie, following him. "Is he back?"

The boy stopped short as he noticed the worried look on his mother's face.

"He won't be long," declared Rita to reassure them and perhaps to reassure herself as well.

That morning, Paul had had to leave for Cascia in spite of the oncoming storm. Since then, nature's elements had broken loose, making certain roads impassable. The members of that small family tried to hide their anxiety from one another, but their fears grew as the hours passed.

In the middle of the night, heavy knocks pounded on the door. James-Anthony ran to open it ahead of Rita, around whom Paul-Marie had instinctively extended a protective arm. She quickly freed herself and saw John, one of their neighbors, stumble in. At the same time, the fury of the squall rushed into the security of the room, bringing with it desolation. The newcomer's clothes were covered with mud, his hair streaming. The distraught look on his face indicated that he had not only braved the elements but that he had also seen something terrible.

"Paul?" Rita asked, as she made the sign of the cross.

"Come quickly. Attacked...near the Corno...an ambush... they fled...."

"Who?"

"I don't know. Let's go get him."

"Dead?"

The neighbor did not answer and bowed his head. Quickly, he picked up his torch and hurried out again with the poor woman. The boys had only time to throw a warm mantle over their mother's shoulders. They then fell into step at some distance, wishing to watch over Rita without annoying her.

When other residents of Rocca-Porena saw lights go by their homes, they quickly came out and joined the group. They sensed that a tragedy had occurred somewhere in this hostile storm. The cheerless procession turned into the path leading to the valley. Rita was silent. She was thinking of Paul, of their good moments together and of their unhappy days. She was earnestly praying for the salvation of his soul.

John was speaking to her in short clipped sentences. "He was still alive at first. He forgave...and he thought of you, of his sons. He was praying...."

Rita's grief was soothed by gratitude to God, who had answered her prayers. Her Paul had died as a good Christian. And he had kept his own in mind until the end. They would meet again in heaven.

But at the end of her sorrowful journey, she became petrified, almost to the point of fainting, when she saw her husband's mutilated body. It took a few minutes before, faithful to her spiritual principles, she was able to offer up her sufferings and those of her beloved Paul, in union with the passion of her Savior.

Her sons, whom she had wanted to spare the sight of their father's blood, were standing a few feet away, firm and resolute. They were whispering indistinct words, among which could be detected: "revenge."

Chapter 4
Alone with God

Who could have planned this ambush—for obviously, this was what it had been—against Paul de Ferdinand, who had gone about unarmed in the deserted valley? Years before he had given up quarrels and brawls and had tried to live at peace with everyone.

But perhaps not everyone had felt inclined to make peace with him. In those troubled times, where blood called for blood, old grudges could die hard, even after successive generations. Who knows the hatred that some family, the descendants of a past enemy, long since gone, could have harbored against him?

This was why Rita felt that a new worry was being added to her grief. Her sons had done their best to assume their father's tasks. They were attentive and loving toward her. But, in spite of their good intentions, they were self-willed. Their independent attitudes made her anxious. They were evading her authority and her chidings. A desire for revenge was rising in them, and they made no attempt to hide it. This desire was fostered by local customs and the remarks of friends and acquaintances. To people who mentioned their father, the adolescents would grimly reply, "We'll get our father's murderers! We won't leave that unpunished!"

"Enough blood, enough tears," the widow would moan. "Surely, I've brought you up with attitudes completely different from these. The Gospel forbids us to take justice into our own hands. Your father forgave as I have forgiven. He would not approve."

But like many other young people, the twins turned a deaf

ear to her advice and warnings. They loved their mother, but they found her meekness too akin to weakness.

"Is this possible?" Rita would repeat in her prayers. "My God, you helped their father overcome his violent nature and evil inclinations. But now, these have shown up in his sons, even though they're disguised as filial devotion. You know that my Paul would not want them to become murderers because of him. But how can they be made to understand that?"

One day, in the depths of her anxieties, she came to the point of formulating a request that was paradoxical in a mother so tender. She prayed "Lord, rather than allow them to carry out this horrible plan, which is growing in them as they grow in years, take them out of this world!"

For Rita the only perspective on life that mattered was the one that opened out into eternity. To prevent her children from offending God, to make their salvation certain, she was ready to sacrifice a part of their earthly existence and to give up the joy of having them close to her.

In the previous century, another mother had expressed the same wish concerning a son who, however, was giving her no cause to worry. Blanche of Castille, speaking of the future St. Louis, would also have preferred him to die rather than commit sin. The young French king was to live out a full span of life on earth and serve as an example and a model. What would life be for James-Anthony and Paul-Marie?

One evening, a few months after Paul's death, James-Anthony came home from the fields, feverish and shivering. Rita nursed him the best she could with fine herbs and infusions according to recipes handed down to her by Amata. The boy moaned and tossed in his bed. He would take only a little milk and honey and was in more and more pain.

Shortly after, Paul-Marie came down with the same sickness. No doubt this was one of the epidemics that raged in that century. Nursing methods were primitive, communicable diseases poorly controlled and sanitation little developed. Once again, like little children, the adolescents groaned as they called, "Mamma! Mamma!"

Their mother was constantly at their side, watching over

them day and night, trying to bring them relief. With the help of a few elderly women of the village, she tried to use remedies that had worked with others. She continually prayed that the outcome might be what was best for them. She hoped to see them come out of this illness alive and converted.

God had decided otherwise. One after the other, they received the Anointing of the Sick, after having whispered while gazing peacefully at the crucifix, "Forgive us as we forgive...."

"Forgive... the assassins of our father," Paul-Marie uttered with difficulty.

And James-Anthony echoed, "No revenge. Forgiveness...."

Rita was sobbing at their bedside, torn between grief and the consolation of having turned them away from evil.

Humanly speaking, she had done everything she could to save them. Now, broken with grief but strengthened in Christian hope, she finally found herself absolutely alone at Rocca-Porena.

———————

"Here comes Rita de Ferdinand back from Cascia."

"How weary and sad she looks."

"That's not surprising after all her bereavements."

Rita was coming up the hill slowly, her head bowed. From time to time, she would make the effort to raise her eyes to acknowledge a greeting from a friend. She would even attempt to smile, but without success. It was not only her misfortunes that bore down upon her this evening, but a terrible disappointment that had been added over and above the rest.

Once she was home again, even before having something to eat, she went to the hard mattress she used as a penance. She just lay there, exhausted. Through the dormer window that she always kept open, she distractedly watched the movement of the stars across the autumn sky. Mentally Rita went over her trying day.

It had begun at the monastery of St. Mary Magdalen, in Cascia, late in the morning. After a long wait, Rita had finally obtained an interview with the mother superior.

Having greeted her with a deep bow according to the

formalities of the time, Rita had settled into a seat to which the abbess had motioned her. The abbess herself was seated behind an imposing desk. When asked to present her request, Rita answered with neither fear nor boldness, "Reverend Mother, I have come to ask your permission to enter your novitiate."

"But how old are you?" exclaimed the superior, who added, "In any case, this will have to be examined in a community meeting."

Then she asked Rita a great number of questions, taking notes while maintaining an inscrutable expression.

To tell the truth, she more or less knew all the answers, for she had often heard about Paul de Ferdinand, his conversion, his tragic death and his children. And she knew about his wife's virtue as well.

"Come back this afternoon, my child," she said at the end of the interrogation. "We will let you know the council's decision."

Rita spent those hours of expectation and hope in prayer at St. Mary's, the church where she had been baptized. She begged fervently that her aspirations might be fulfilled. Then she stood again in front of the heavy door surmounted by a cross.

Again, the parlor, the bare little room, the reverent bows to the abbess.

Unconsciously playing with the goose-feather pen on her writing desk, the abbess spoke, slowly and with feeling. Her words sounded hopeful to Rita. "My dear child," she began, "I do not question your sincerity. I am also aware of your faith and your works of charity. The trials you have just experienced deserve some consideration."

Her heart beating with excitement, Paul's widow could already see herself admitted among the novices. She was about to give thanks to God in her heart when the abbess said something that dampened her enthusiasm. Perhaps she had rejoiced too soon?

"However," the worthy sister continued, "however, that is not enough."

"There we are!" thought Rita, sighing within herself.

"Other conditions will have to be met...delays...proofs that I have a vocation. No doubt, as well, inquiries made by higher authorities, what else? I am ready to accept, to agree to everything, to wait patiently as long as necessary, provided I reach my goal."

"For all that," continued the mother abbess, "these very tribulations are an obstacle to the fulfillment of your wish. They are an obstacle...how shall I express it? An absolute one, I am sorry to say."

The abbess did not dare look at the woman, huddled up on her chair and holding back her tears. In spite of her stern appearance, the Reverend Mother detested being a cause of grief. But sometimes one had to appear insensitive.

Rita did not realize what was happening to her. She must have misunderstood, she thought. Trembling, she dared to murmur, "Mother, you don't mean that never...?"

"You see that I am as grieved about this as you are yourself, my child. My dear child, I would have loved to welcome you. But, since its foundation, our congregation has been exclusively reserved for young girls. A person who has known marriage and motherhood—even if these were lived in a Christian spirit according to the precepts of our holy Church, such a person could never find her place here. Our sisters in assembly were definite on that point."

Noting that her visitor remained in shock, as it were, the superior added, while going through the motions of a blessing, "Believe me, I am deeply sorry, my dear daughter. You certainly would have been an honest and fervent religious. But we must not act against the rules, not against the custom. May God watch over you in the world. We shall pray for you."

The interview had come to an end. Rita still did not know how she had managed to come back to Rocca-Porena, for she had been guided by instinct alone. She neither saw the setting sun, nor felt the biting north wind. Her heart was much too heavy!

And, in the night, the memory of this unfruitful initiative kept her awake, and in tears, for a long time. The full, round moon was casting a silver shimmer across the sky of Umbria, as it had cast its silver shimmer long ago on the Mount of Olives during the agony of the Master.

But to think that only one refusal could discourage Rita would be to misjudge her. Sometime later, she renewed her request. After a consultation among the members of the community—purely formal, she felt—the answer was the same. "We cannot accept widows," the abbess repeated. "We are sorry."

The abbess sensed the devastating effects the refusal had on Rita's weary body and tired heart. She appeared yet thinner than previously and more hurt. But, strangely enough she remained as determined as ever to pursue her impossible dream.

"My dear child," the abbess told Rita as she was leading her out, "your vocation could flourish somewhere else, perhaps. There are other monasteries in Cascia."

No, it was here, in the St. Mary Magdalen monastery that Rita was bent on entering. She vaguely felt that was the only place she would be able to serve the Lord as he should be served. An irresistible impulse drove her to this monastery and to no other.

The poor woman presented her petition a third time and met with the same refusal. This time, the abbess did not take the trouble to consult the sisters. She insinuated that she would not agree to meet this obstinate widow anymore.

And yet, Rita clearly felt that she "must" become a member of the community which was rejecting her relentlessly. The words of the Gospel were vivid in her mind and in her heart: "Knock, and it shall be opened to you" (cf Mt 7:7).

Since it was useless to knock at this forbidding door, she would turn once more to heaven. Because she had obtained graces of conversion for her own, she had the feeling that the "impossibilities" of this earth could become realities, upon her fervent request.

Nevertheless, this time, the obstacle was of some proportion. Was God trying to make her understand that she had been mistaken in believing that, from all eternity, she had been destined to a monastic life?

Chapter 5

Beyond the Impossible

Rita did not lose heart. She kept on praying and doing good around her. Once she had overcome the effects of her disappointment, she began to smile again and to hope against all hope.

So that she might be more available when the hour chosen by God would strike, she gradually sold all her possessions, keeping only a place to sleep. The money she had collected would go to the community when she would join it—if this community which persisted in rejecting her really needed some gifts. Indeed, Paul's widow still deserved her nickname, *the woman without a grudge*.

But the St. Mary Magdalen monastery also had a great need of vocations, Rita thought. If it would be God's will, she would enter there when the time came, in spite of the superior, in spite of the nun's council, in spite of the whole world! It was a matter of waiting. The decision was not hers.

One evening, Rita was at home praying. Winter had begun to set in. A bitter north wind was blowing through the denuded trees and howling down the chimney.

Suddenly, a voice called from outside, "Rita! Rita!"

The recluse interrupted her prayer, ran to the gable window, and looked down the street. She saw no one. The huge olive tree in the neighbors' garden was writhing and twisting in the squall. She thought she had heard the sound of a human voice, but this was undoubtedly the fruit of her imagination.

However, a few minutes later, when she had returned to her prayer, she heard again, more distinctly this time, "Rita! Rita!"

There were no more doubts. Someone needed her urgently. It was probably a neighboring woman whom she had not been able to detect in the shadows the first time.

She opened the door and found an oddly-dressed man on her doorstep. He wore primitive apparel made of the skins of animals, had long hair and wore a strap around his waist. Why yes, this was like the pictures and statues representing St. John the Baptist, the precursor, one of the saints she prayed to most frequently.

The mysterious visitor motioned to her, and Rita, very impressed but trusting, put on her cloak and followed him. They walked out of the sleeping village, among the swirls of dust stirred up by the gusts of wind, and came to the rock of Rocca-Porena. It was an ominous place on this dark night. One could barely make out the outline of the gray rock rising against the turbulent sky. Rita had never come here after nightfall.

And now suddenly, the poor woman could move forward no more. In front of her, the ground had opened up, disclosing a terrifying abyss. Shaking from head to foot, she entrusted her soul to God.

Rita was right in having recourse to the supreme protection. There were three guides now, taking her along the rocky road leading to Cascia, beyond the obstacle that she had crossed she knew not how. In front of her, along with St. John the Baptist were two other guides, whom she also recognized as familiar saints of her prayers: St. Augustine and St. Nicholas of Tolentino, as they appeared in popular imagery.

A little later, Rita came to her senses and saw that the three saints had disappeared. But she also discovered with a joy mingled with wonder, that she was within the walls of St. Mary Magdalen monastery. And all the gates were closed.

This time the nuns would have to accept her, since God himself had had someone lead her there.

"Reverend Mother! Look! Someone is in my stall!"

In spite of the rigorous rule of silence practiced in the chapel, Sister Angelina had not been able to hold back this hushed exclamation. As she had been about to take her place for the first morning Office, she had been surprised to find there a stranger, a woman dressed as a villager, lost in deep prayer. She referred the matter to her superior as discreetly as amazement and fright allowed.

The abbess came near, skeptical, ready to scold the yet half-asleep novice. But by the weak light of the candles she had to yield to the fact that a woman whose features she could not make out was indeed there and seemed oblivious to what was going on around her.

The nuns, in their ranks, were getting excited. They whispered to each other, not knowing what to make of this extraordinary event. The reverend mother beckoned to the sister who was in charge of the doors. She proceeded with a quick interrogation, whispered but thorough.

"Sister Carola, are you absolutely sure that you securely locked all the doors of the monastery last night?"

"Why yes, Reverend Mother, as usual."

"You will understand that I wish to check."

The tone of voice admitted no reply. Head bowed, the old sister, convinced she had scrupulously fulfilled her duty, nevertheless followed the abbess with apprehension. Would she have to make a severe penance for an oversight of which she was not guilty? All the apparent evidence was against her. After all, she too had seen the woman with her own eyes! To reach the choir, the intruder would have had to come through some entrance. How had she been able to outwit the intricacies of the bolts and chains? Traces of the break-in had to be obvious somewhere.

"Oh! See for yourself, Reverend Mother. All is well barred, just as I left it yesterday. I knew very well that...."

"That is enough, my child. I accept your good faith. Let us join the sisters again."

Relieved and intrigued at the same time, the older sister retraced her steps down the dark hallways, following her superior. In vain, the superior was trying to unravel this mystery. She found the intruding woman still in the same place as before. The woman stood up and bowed in respect. Why, yes, it was Rita, that obstinate widow who had been put off three times! Now she was making another attempt. They could not get rid of her. By what means, in defiance of all human logic, had she come where she should not be?

"How did you dare overrule our refusal?" asked the superior in a sharp tone of voice.

Her offended expression and her harsh voice would have frightened anyone else but Rita. She simply replied matter-of-factly, "The Lord wanted it this way, Reverend Mother."

"An illusion of yours! But, tell me, whoever let you in, despite the security of our cloister?"

"St. John the Baptist, St. Nicholas of Tolentino and St. Augustine, Reverend Mother."

The reverend mother superior of the Augustinian Sisters of St. Mary Magdalen was, of course, open to the supernatural. But to this point? On the other hand, she knew that this woman had already displayed a strong determination and an ardent desire for monastic life. There was nothing of the brazen or self-deluded about her.

Having recovered her temper to some extent, the superior demanded further explanations and gathered all the community in an adjacent room. Rita was asked to give a detailed account of her experience; she did so, simply and convincingly. Anything could be expected in the light of faith.

"What do you think of all this, sisters?" asked the superior when Rita had finished her story. "Do you see the finger of God in this as I do?"

All the sisters bowed their heads in agreement. Rita, who had remained standing in the middle of the group like an accused criminal waiting for the judge's verdict, felt she had won the match. Or rather, heaven had won it for her.

The abbess spoke solemnly. "Very well," she said. "We shall not act against the will of God. Rita de Ferdinand, we declare that you are admitted into our novitiate. You will be called Sister Rita. And now, sisters, let us return to the chapel. *Praise the Lord.*"

The whole community began to sing the psalm of praise. Then the Office proceeded on as it did every morning, delayed only by the "exceptional circumstances." Last in the line of novices, the newly-arrived recruit prayed with fervor. For the first time in many years, Rita had the feeling that at last she was comfortably where Providence wished her to be. As a result of all this, would she experience peace and happiness?

Certainly not! Besides, she did not aspire to that. Since her childhood days, she had wanted to unite herself as intimately as possible to the passion of Christ. With this in mind, she had accepted with a Christian spirit the trials encountered in the world. When she had wished to enter the monastery, it was to be closer to Jesus and not to be shielded from difficulties.

The time spent in the novitiate represents a period of difficult adjustment for all candidates, even when they are young. The hushed atmosphere of those times, the duties to perform within the community, the forms of prayer were to some extent difficult for a newcomer, however fervent she might have been. Her personality, already formed in other ways, had to be adapted to what she was called to become, according to the demands made by her vocation. When the novice was forty years old, and had kept her own house, as a wife and mother, the shift between the two worlds was yet more marked.

To be sure, Rita now saw the realization of her dearest wish, which had become all the more persistent for having been thwarted for so many years. She could miss nothing of the outside world, since she had not left those she loved behind, but was to find them in days to come near the Lord. This was where she would reach them again, in prayer first.

Rita's former life had accustomed her to put into practice what she must now solemnly promise to do.

For a long time, she had accustomed herself to obey, first to her aged parents and then to a domineering husband, as well as to accept circumstances of all sorts which had imposed heavy burdens upon her.

The spirit of poverty was not unknown to Rita who, as a little girl, had refused ribbons. As an adolescent, she had deprived herself for the sake of the unfortunate. As Paul's wife, she had been bent on secretly denying herself.

Regarding chastity, Rita had always felt strongly attracted to that virtue. Even as a married woman, she had always given priority to the love of God. At the time of her widowhood, she had given up human love.

On the other hand, her age constituted a more serious handicap. She felt "old" among her fellow sisters, some of whom did not hesitate to remind her of her age. At times, it seemed to her that she should not stay there, that she had made a mistake in wanting, at all costs, to mingle with the young novices. And yet, the saints could not have misled her by bringing her to the St. Mary Magdalen monastery.

Rita was very much in touch with reality while she was trying to overcome these obstacles. Thus, she wanted to assume the more difficult tasks, so as to relieve the sisters who were more feeble or of poorer health. Never, she thought, would she be able to measure up to them in purity and in prayer. It was fair that she should try to compensate in some other way.

Meanwhile, the devil was keeping watch—jealous of the good in her, of the souls she had snatched away from him, of those she would yet snatch away from him, unless he were careful. He would inflict upon her temptations to despair, to pride, to impurity—temptations that she had never known in the world. Nevertheless, being energetic and convinced about her vocation, as well as sure of divine protection, Rita overcame these afflictions. Patience, perseverance, penances to subdue the mind and body, untiring charity—these were the weapons she would use in her fight against Satan.

Her superior was firm with her. Impressed by the circumstances of Rita's admission into the community, she had a feeling that this was a choice recruit whose spiritual ascent and moral progress must be wrought in trials—sometimes uncalled for trials.

"Sister Rita!"

"Reverend Mother?"

"Take this bucket and come with me to the garden."

Without a word, the novice went about this task. The pail she filled at the pump was heavy. The path was endless. Perhaps, in her mind, Rita was seeing another garden again, one where two small children had toddled along beside her? Or again, that of her childhood home, the Casa Lotti, fragrant with the scents of Amata's flowers?

She finally came to a withered branch staked in the ground in a remote corner of the flowerbed.

"You will water this plant regularly, Sister Rita, twice a day—in the morning after the Office and in the evening before Vespers. Don't fail to do so. I especially insist on this!"

Humanly speaking, what could be the use of this silly task? Obviously, this tree had no roots, it would slowly rot under these useless drops of water.

But Rita quietly obeyed without questioning. If the abbess was asking her to fulfill this task, perhaps she was wasting her time from the standpoint of gardening, but certainly not from the spiritual point of view. To be sure, this useless exercise would teach her patience and self-discipline.

As for the dead branch, it would never come to life again.

Chapter 6

Totally Committed Religious

Already strong in the early morning, the sun was beating down on the white walls of the cloister, casting its golden rays between the arches. Under the arcade, a procession was making its way toward the chapel. Among the novices who were taking their vows on that day, Rita, with joy in her heart, was turning her thoughts to God. After so many obstacles, circuitous ways and delays, her goal, pursued in vain for so long, was at last within her reach. In a few moments, she would be the spouse of Jesus in actual fact, as she already was in her heart!

The ceremony unfolded with a ritual simplicity that enhanced its dignity. When her turn came, after her companions who had been in the monastery for a longer time than she, Rita knelt, answered, affirmed, promised. She promised obedience to the rule of the order and to the abbess, who clasped Rita's joined hands in one of her own as she placed her other hand on Rita's head. This gesture on the part of the superior symbolized both authority and protection. Through her, the newly-professed nuns gave themselves to Jesus forever.

According to custom, this commitment had to be witnessed by an official delegated by civil authorities—that is, a notary. Seated in the first place among those attending the ceremony, the notary was absentmindedly following the event. This was tantamount to professional routine for him. Of course, he whispered a prayer for the newly professed sisters. He did not know that the account he would write on parchment this time would live on through centuries. In his eyes, as in those of everyone else, the nun who would henceforth bear the name Sister Rita was simply a nun like any of the others. She was in a monastery similar to all other monasteries, lost in the midst of these mountains beyond which the name Cascia had not yet traveled.

In the midst of the crowd, voices from Rocca-Porena were whispering.

"She is Paul de Ferdinand's widow, Antonio and Amata's daughter."

"You know, the little girl who took so long in coming, who would nurse me so tenderly when she was fifteen."

"What an idea for her to have become a nun!"

"She had some difficult times with poor Paul. May God rest his soul."

"And grief, bereavements..."

"At last, she has found a refuge; the poor woman was left all alone!"

No, Rita had not come here to escape solitude or human sorrows. She had come here, very simply, because she loved.

Back in her cell on the evening of this unforgettable day, Rita was not trying to fall asleep. She had the habit of prolonging her prayer until sheer fatigue would close her eyes. An ardent piety was joined to her inborn taste for mortification. This evening, more than ever, she needed to worship, to give thanks, and also to contemplate the passion of her Spouse as a newly-professed sister, so as to share it more intimately.

When emotions and weariness finally overcame her, she had a strange dream.

Our Lord appeared to her. He was holding up an immense ladder, the upper steps of which were lost in the dazzling clouds of heaven. The newly-professed sister immediately understood the symbolic meaning of this vision. Henceforth, while leaning on Christ, she would have to climb the steps to perfection to reach intimate union with God in paradise.

Obviously, this would not come about without struggles and sacrifices. The monastery was not an automatic guarantee of holiness. It simply offered a setting favorable to sanctity's development, provided the soul lent itself to its growth. This would not be accomplished without difficulties. When she awakened, Sister Rita made up her mind that she would increase her efforts to climb, little by little, this spiritual ladder of which she had been so providentially given a glimpse.

The rule that was to guide the sisters of St. Mary Magdalen on the way to perfection was that of St. Augustine. After the persecutions in Africa during the first centuries of Christianity, the hermits who had drawn inspiration from this rule had taken refuge in Europe and a few had come precisely to Italy. They had given rise to the small sanctuaries scattered throughout the mountains of Umbria. The Augustinian rule was also observed in many monasteries of women.

This was the reason why, at Rita's time, St. Augustine and his followers were particularly venerated in this country. Special veneration was paid to St. Nicholas of Tolentino, one of the three who had brought Rita into the cloister. When she was still very small, Rita had been attracted to Augustinian spirituality, and so in the monastery she found herself on familiar grounds.

At the beginning of the fifteenth century, strict enclosure of the community was not yet compulsory as it would be later, after the Council of Trent. The nuns could go out and mingle with the residents of the city to bring help to the poor and the sick. A number of these came to the very steps of St. Mary Magdalen monastery every morning to beg or to show their sores. Sister Rita was one of the most devoted to them. No pain, physical or moral, would dishearten her. As she had always done since her youth, she deprived herself to give more to those who were hungry and was unsparing of her time, her trouble, her comforting smile.

Of course, she would not neglect her religious duties for all that. When she was not in deep prayer or reciting the Divine Office, she was doing good works inside or outside the monastery, for her sisters were also of concern to her. She kept the least appetizing dishes for herself and took upon herself the most exhausting extra duties. She dressed in clothes that were very worn. She knew how to console and to give courage when necessary. And so, people around her often asked her for advice.

"Sister Rita, two men insulted us on the way this morning, as we were coming out of that old blind woman's house, in the alley near St. Mary's."

"Don't pay any attention. Jesus, too, was insulted! What matters is to do good."

"Sister, I cough and cough. I will never be well again. What will become of my family?"

"Set your mind at ease, my friend. God will take care of your family and of you as well. Here, take this medication. It will help you get rid of that bad cold."

The voice was gentle; so was the hand. The poor learned to know this sister who was so compassionate. Many of the nuns loved her as well and acknowledged her merit. Not all of them, however. There, as everywhere else, some characters were touchy. There were misunderstandings.

"What does she have that we don't have, that Rita?"

"Soon everything in Cascia will be her doing!"

An exaggeration, possibly? And yet, it was true that Sister Rita's name was on the lips of the people in the city. They blessed it and thereby blessed God.

The person concerned hardly suspected anything of the sort. When echoes of praise reached Rita, this only put her in a state of utter embarrassment. In all humility, she wanted to fight against her shortcomings, against the evil inclinations of nature and against the devil, ever ready to attack someone who, more than ever, was becoming his enemy.

At times of violent assaults, Rita went so far as to burn or scourge herself. Sometimes the sisters would meet her in the corridors of the monastery, going in the direction of her cell. If someone who was more inquisitive than the others would ask where she was going at this time of day, she would reply, "I am going to fight my enemy." This might be translated as: she was retiring to her cell to scourge herself.

After Rita died, it was discovered that under her clothes she had worn a hairshirt interwoven with thorns. Her principles of spirituality were always the same: self-denial, mortification, union with the passion of Christ. Satan would eventually understand that he would never get the best of her and that he would have to withdraw. But this would take years. Meanwhile Rita never lost heart.

The vow of obedience did not seem to be a problem for

Rita. And yet, we do not know whether she ever grew inwardly impatient in face of certain demands made by monastic life. Who can know the depths of the heart? Among the young sisters, Rita obviously had had the most experience. She had run her own home, taken care of her children. Here she had to submit in all things and ask permission for the least action slightly out of the ordinary. She also had to lend herself to those useless obligations the superior had imposed upon her to mold her character. To begin with, there was that twig of dead wood she had to water twice a day.

It was late afternoon. The heat was heavy. The sun darted strong rays across the dusty vegetation. All that could be heard was the strident noise of the cicadas. Sister Rita walked with a heavy step, her arms and legs worn out. Since Matins, she had answered so many calls, bent her knees so often while serving the Lord, the poor, and the community, that she felt weary, so weary. She could well do without this extra task! The path to the far end of the garden was long. The bucket was heavy. And why all this? Humanly speaking, it was all for nothing. No, it was to fulfill the duty of obedience. *Deo Gratias* (Thanks be to God) in spite of everything.

At the turn of one of the lanes, Rita met two of her sisters who were pacing up and down while saying their Office. When they saw her, they exchanged ironic glances. They made a half-turn in the front of the large cypress tree, caught up to Rita, passed her and preceded her to the meeting point of the garden paths where the dead stick had been planted. Obviously, they would be there as if by chance to watch Rita laboring strenuously with her bucket in a sheer waste of time and energy.

Painfully, Rita neared the stick, set down the pail for a moment to catch her breath and picked it up again.

Exclamations of surprise made her look up. In front of her, the dead wood, which had still been dried up that morning, was decked with branches that had turned green again. Small leaves were beginning to entwine around the sap-filled twigs. The worthless stock had come to life again and was becoming a vine that would bear fruit in due season.

Her two companions, who had discovered the wonder

before she had, were muttering jumbled words of embarrassment. Then, like two darts, they dashed toward the community,
on the way dropping an Office book on the gravel path.

A few minutes later, the superior, having been told of the
wonder, came to the vine with all the sisters who, at that
moment, were free and able to follow her. She had not had the
heart to send them back to their tasks or to their prayers. Once
again, a hymn of praise rose up to the Lord.

And Sister Rita? What did she think of this divine favor?
With her customary humility, she remembered only the lesson
of obedience, of trust and perseverance emerging from this
astounding incident. Not for one moment did she suspect that
her virtue might have had something to do with this. As far as
she was concerned, another sister doing the same thing would
have "obtained" the same results. As soon as she was able to slip
away, she simply resumed her task of peeling vegetables in the
kitchen. She was giving a helping hand to the sister cook, who
was not well that day.

The following day, the people of Cascia and the surround-
ing area had but one topic of conversation: "Sister Rita's vine."
The plant continued to grow and spread its branches. Sometime
later, magnificent clusters of sweet grapes would be hanging on
those branches. The community would treat itself to them with
reverence, putting the best aside for the poor. Let us not mention
Sister Rita, who would taste them only in obedience and take her
share to those whose well-being depended upon her.

During the days following this incident, Rita drew the
substance for her meditations from the parable of the *True Vine*.
Oh, how she wished she could pour the sap of divine grace into
souls as the Master did!

Chapter 7

With the Crucified Jesus

Since the time long past when, on Amata's knees, Rita would throw kisses to the crucifix, she had always felt close to the passion of our Lord. Now that she was a religious, it was the main topic of her meditations.

One day, during one of these intimate conversations, her soul was especially attracted by words that she had certainly read many times: "*I am the way, the truth and the life*" (cf Jn 14:16).

From that moment on, she would try to apply them in her devotion to Jesus on the cross. Indeed, to reach the perfection that had become her goal since the day of her profession, she would follow the way of Jesus—that is, the way of the cross. In this way she was sure of finding the truth and of attaining the only true life. In union with Mary, she would stay as close as possible to the cross in thought and prayer, in contemplation and sacrifice.

In her imagination, she had arranged several stages of the passion in her cell. Here was the tribunal. There, Calvary. Before this form of devotion became established in the Church, Rita had a feeling for it and practiced what was to become the Way of the Cross. She would move from one to another of these sorrowful stations, which stirred within her stronger and stronger feelings of compassion. She would visualize them in her mind with such heart-gripping vividness that she felt as if she herself were being martyred with our Lord.

"Sister Rita is not up yet. Could she be ill?" the sisters asked each other one morning as they were assembling for Office.

"She really would have to be seriously ill, for she is so hard on herself!" the anxious superior thought. And quickly she dispatched one of the sisters to the cell of the absentee. The messenger returned almost immediately, calling in dismay, "Mother! Mother! She is dead! Sister Rita is dead! I found her lying on the floor, unconscious and pale, so pale!"

The abbess rushed out and, indeed, found Rita lying on the floor, motionless, her complexion pasty. Dead? Not really; she had only fainted. Near her, a primitive kind of scourge made up of small chains explained her fainting spell—scourging voluntarily inflicted upon herself for too long and with too much vigor.

Rita would scourge herself three times a day to do penance for intentions dear to her heart—first for the deceased, then for sinners and finally for all the benefactors of the monastery.

The superior and sisters carried Rita to her mattress, revived her and urged her to use more discretion in her mortifications. Then, upon Rita's insistent request, the superior brought her back among her sisters, who were upset and murmuring about the incident.

"Will this Rita, unobtrusive as she is, always be a source of surprise and trouble?" thought the good mother as she firmly motioned to her little flock to calm down. "Can't she do anything as the others do?"

No, Sister Rita was not an ordinary religious. And, time and again, she would startle the people around her with fainting spells brought on by her excessively harsh manner of practicing penance. Little by little, those near her would grow accustomed to this. But, sometime later, without wishing to do so, she became a source of deeper disturbance for the community.

The year was 1443. Important news was spreading in Cascia. The Lenten sermons, soon to begin, would be preached this year at St. Mary's by a well-known Franciscan, James della Marca. He was a companion of Bernardine of Siena and John Capistran, both of whom, like himself, would eventually be canonized. At that time James della Marca was especially known for the vivid and convincing style he had brought to the art of preaching—which until then had been somewhat abstract. Everyone, or almost everyone, rushed to hear him.

The nuns of St. Mary Magdalen were among these. Their

rule, which allowed them to go out of the cloister to do good works, also let them take part in certain devotions outside the monastery. The untiring preacher spoke for hours in the ice-cold church. Everyone was hanging onto his words, and no one found the time long or felt the cold. No one including Rita.

It was Good Friday. With impassioned words and forceful gestures, the preacher described the passion of the Lord as he brandished a crucifix in front of the congregation. He particularly insisted on our Christ's abandonment by his apostles and disciples, by the multitude of the so-called "faithful" of all times. And he exalted John and Mary Magdalen who, along with Mary, the mother of Jesus, had been the only ones to offer Jesus some consolation. These were models to follow and imitate.

Rita was literally overwhelmed by the vivid scene of the passion, even though she had called it to her own mind time and again. She had never heard it described in such powerful terms.

She was still pondering this as she climbed back up to the monastery on this misty evening after the procession that had concluded the Office. She offered the sharp climb in union with Jesus on the road to Calvary. She was already over sixty and her strength was waning.

That did not prevent her from hurrying to the monastery chapel, where she lost herself in a long meditative prayer at the foot of the cross. It seemed to her that the bleeding wounds of Christ were imprinted in her and that she could feel their pain. But she wanted to go further. "O Jesus," she whispered fervently, "I beg you, I entreat you, grant that at least *one* of these thorns that are bruising your forehead so cruelly may come and bruise mine. Let me really have a part, however slight, in your passion."

The crucifix was large; it took up a whole section of the wall. Sister Rita humbly remained in front of it, her head bowed. Suddenly a thorn of plaster, one that made up the crown in the fresco, began to break loose. It fell and lodged itself in the forehead of the prostrate sister. This was a severe shock for Rita. She reeled and fell unconscious from the intermingled pain and joy.

She stayed there a long time. Then, when she had regained consciousness and strength in the silence and darkness of the night, she made her way to her cell, where she ended the night in acts of thanksgiving.

The next morning, in the semi-darkness of the chapel, the sisters did not immediately notice the strange wound. But a little later, in the dining room, her neighbor at table suddenly drew away from Rita while holding her nose. The other sisters also looked at her with interest and a certain disgust. The wound was spreading on her forehead and from it flowed, not bright red blood, but an evil-smelling darkish pus. Once again, the superior was alarmed.

She was becoming accustomed to Sister Rita's supernatural adventures. For this reason, after having questioned her in private, the abbess hardly hesitated to believe her. Besides, the proof was there.

However, the sisters could see and smell the wound. They soon felt uncomfortable when near Rita's gaping sore, which was perhaps—some were still in doubt—of heavenly origin, but which gave off a foul stench. Some now openly held their noses when Rita came near. Others avoided her like the plague. She had to have her meals by herself at the end of the table and had to pray apart from the others.

This was still not enough. She was to share the moral humiliations of the crucified Jesus to the utmost. She would soon be totally cast aside.

"My child," the abbess told her one evening, "from this day on, you will remain in your cell. One of your sisters will bring your meals to you. For the Offices, you will remain at the back of the chapel. You will receive Communion after the other sisters."

The abbess was somewhat uncomfortable to have to inflict these stern commands upon such an exemplary sister—commands which could have been taken as undeserved penance. But she was responsible for the whole flock. The common good must not be sacrificed for the sake of a particular situation.

Besides, the mother superior knew very well that Sister Rita understood, agreed, offered it up. As the abbess cast a kindly glance at Rita, one could have detected compassion mixed with admiration. Burdened by the weight of years and worries, the abbess returned to the duties of her office. Being abbess in the convent of St. Mary Magdalen of Cascia, in this year of 1443, obviously was not easy.

A few years went by. Pope Eugene IV had died and Nicholas V had succeeded him. Pope Nicholas undertook the delicate task of reorganizing the Church after the years of schism and the papal exile at Avignon. Those unfortunate incidents belonging to an already distant past had left traces in their wake: divisions and ruins—both material and moral.

Because he was favored by better circumstances than his predecessors had been, since the Italian Peninsula was enjoying relative peace, the new Pope wished to attract a large number of Catholics to Rome. By means of a jubilee, he wanted the Christians to work toward their salvation and to inject some saintliness into the world. To achieve this, he declared 1450 a Holy Year. The Pope granted a plenary indulgence to those who would go on pilgrimage to the Eternal City, on condition that a few particular practices, visits to basilicas and ritual prayers be observed. He had many religious buildings restored to welcome the visitors and, among other initiatives, he asked the artist Fra Angelico to paint some frescoes.

In those days, news would spread only by means of travelers going about on foot or horseback. Consequently, the papal messages took a long time to reach the parishes. Nevertheless, news of the approaching opening of the Holy Year eventually came to Cascia and echoes of it reached the walls of St. Mary Magdalen monastery. What a unique opportunity to see the Holy Father and to promote one's own salvation!

Over and above this, while religious fervor was to benefit from this pilgrimage, nothing prevented the pilgrim from considering the human aspect of things as well. Just think! Here was the opportunity to leave, not only the monastery, but also the city, even the province. It meant to travel about and see new faces, to know the wonders of Rome, to retrace the footsteps of the early Christians. That was enough to set more than one nun off into flights of fancy. "May I be part of our delegation," each sister said to herself. So Rita thought, as did the others. For her, however, the motive remained purely spiritual. There would be merits to be earned, a papal blessing to receive and holy relics to venerate.

With neither fear nor boldness, Rita asked permission to join the sisters who would be making this trip. She received the reply she had expected. "My child," said the abbess, "I understand your wish. But you will surely sense how impossible it is for me to allow you to go about in the world among your sisters with a wound so...obvious."

"...and evil-smelling. I know, Reverend Mother. However, if...."

"The only condition would be that your wound heal before it is time to leave. In that case, I would not go against your wish."

Rita made no response. But her eyes were more eloquent than words. Healing was unlikely, especially in so short a time, but she did not despair of obtaining it. Perhaps God would like her to go to Rome, too.

The abbess remained deep in thought. This sister had appeared so sure of herself, as if she knew the secrets of heaven. It was true enough that Rita had already obtained so many unhoped-for favors through her simple faith. Her prayer had triumphed over the impossible so many times! Why not again this time?

The abbess was, therefore, only half taken by surprise when, a few days before the date set for the departure of the delegation, Sister Rita came to her one morning with her forehead smooth, cleared from all signs of the wound. Again, heaven had heard her call. The application of a very ordinary ointment had quickly dried up the sore. There was one reservation, however: the wound would reappear immediately after Rita's return to Cascia. This was the pact she had made with the Lord. And no one knew that she had asked that only the visible mark of her stigmata disappear, not the pain. If the thorn remained invisible, the throbbing pain was always there. What of it? She could now set out on her journey to Rome. Her heart was filled with gratitude.

And so, one morning a small group of sisters, fired with enthusiasm, crossed the threshold of the monastery to set out on an expedition which would have many emotional moments.

Chapter 8

All Roads Lead to Rome

The Superior of the St. Mary Magdalen monastery put the oldest and wisest of her daughters, Sister Rita, at the head of the small delegation.

Weakened by her sixty years and by continual self-denial, Sister Rita would no doubt suffer more than the others during this arduous trip. But no one would know anything about that. To her own weariness would be added the task of watching over her sisters.

She organized the material supplies for the small group in the best way she could. But Rita would not have been true to herself if she had exercised this responsibility according to human norms.

When they set out, the abbess gave each one a small amount of money to meet her needs along the way. Hardly had the steeples of Cascia disappeared beyond the horizon than one of the sisters began to worry.

"Will we have enough to last to the end of the trip? Rome is far away! What will become of us if we run out of food?"

At this moment, the party was crossing the bridge spanning the Corno, the familiar river that brought back so many memories to Rita. Turning about abruptly, the woman who had been Paul de Ferdinand's wife reached down deep into her monastic pockets and drew out the few coins which had been given to her personally. Casually, she tossed them into the running stream. Cries of surprise and indignation rose from her sisters.

"Oh! Sister Rita!"

"What are you doing there?"

"Have faith in Providence," replied the unperturbed Rita, who was to become *the saint of the impossible.*

Let us imagine these women, deprived of any means of self-defense, suddenly leaving the peaceful atmosphere of their monastery and their small city, launching out, walking along the highroads. The journey disrupted their lifestyle and exposed them to the elements, to accidents, to unpleasant encounters. In any case, they were forced to walk for hours and to sleep and eat randomly at uncertain stopping places.

As they went on, the sisters realized that Rita had been right in not worrying about the following days. Their stops were made at the mercy of circumstances, in convents or in private homes opened to pilgrims. Sometimes, however, they had to sleep out in the open and to subsist on little. Yet, never did they lack the strictly essential minimum. When they had exhausted their means, some unforeseen help or offer of food and accommodations always came up.

However, the enticement of change and adventure began to wear off with the length and difficulties of the trip. Each one had brought along her own personal temperament and reacted accordingly when faced with problems of health or character. The group made its way slowly, praying or singing hymns to suit the moment. But, at the stopping places, the sisters were allowed to converse, and then complaints were brought to light. One had sore feet; another thought she could see bandits lurking everywhere. And so, at times, proper or inopportune, they would have recourse to Rita for protection, for advice and for the settlement of differences.

"I haven't the strength to go on, Sister Rita."

"Sister Rita, do you hear that howling in the woods?"

Or this or that sister would complain that on the previous night one of her traveling companions had kept her from sleeping by reciting her prayers out loud.

Rita would reassure, pacify, offer her arm to the more weary and give courage to the more apprehensive.

On the other hand, as time went on, the younger sisters tended somewhat to relax their usual discipline and to chat indiscriminately with their hosts or with other travelers. Rita would reprimand them, gently but firmly. "Sisters," she would say, "we must conduct ourselves outside of the closure as we do within. For want of the possibility of withdrawing to our cells or to our chapel, we can withdraw within ourselves. Let us speak to others only in cases of necessity or of charity. And let us offer our discomforts to our Lord, who had to bear with much worse."

The pilgrimage route seemed endless. If all roads lead to Rome, those of the fifteenth century were particularly tortuous, rough and difficult. One had to climb mountainsides, descend into valleys and cross rivers on shaky bridges, or make long detours to find a place to wade across.

Slow to come, spring alternated rain with sunshine. Then, suddenly, a heat wave moved in, making the walk more and more painful.

At last, on a beautiful May evening, alive with the strident noise of the cicadas and the twitters of swooping swallows, Rita and her sisters reached one of the hills overlooking the Eternal City. Spontaneously, they broke into a chorus, singing a hymn of thanksgiving to the Lord for having guided them safely to their destination.

A few would have liked to enter the city right away. Now that they were so close to their goal, they were eager to begin their pilgrimage. If Rita had been alone, she would immediately have rushed to the sanctuaries, or even journeyed there on her knees. But, being conscious of her responsibilities, she insisted that her sisters rest and recuperate before joining the crowds and fulfilling the tiring prescriptions of the Jubilee. She easily found a monastery open to pilgrims where each one would regain her strength while looking forward to the next day.

The sisters from Cascia entered Rome by way of the Via Flaminia. They had already had a panoramic view of the huge city. The cupola of St. Peter's did not yet exist, and at that time the basilica was made up of only five naves of ancient construction. Later, these would be replaced by a new, more majestic edifice. Nevertheless, this large church impressed the travelers enormously. This was where they would enter, first of all, to begin their devotions with a prayer on the tomb of the apostles' leader.

They approached this sacred place with indescribable emotion. In spite of the long wait and the trampling of feet, they appreciated the grace granted to them at the conclusion of so many difficulties—the grace to immerse themselves in the wellsprings of the Church, to discover memories and traces of the saints and martyrs. In this way, Rita, especially, could better gauge the solid foundation of the bond woven between Jesus on the cross and his people on earth.

But what most moved Rita's heart and enraptured her with love and sorrow were the instruments of the passion displayed in St. Peter's for the Jubilee.

She almost fainted as she contemplated with dread the spear used by a Roman soldier to pierce the side of Jesus on the cross to make sure that he was really dead.

"Yes, Lord," she murmured to herself, "yes, you really gave up your life amid atrocious tortures. For us... For me..."

She took part in this suffering more deeply than ever, for at this moment the thorn, which was always secretly piercing her, brought on excruciating pains, very difficult to bear. Naturally, Rita began meditating on the mystery of the redemption, oblivious to the pilgrims who urged her to move on, to her sisters tugging at her sleeve and whispering, "Sister Rita, we can't stay here. People are pushing us. We're blocking the way."

Finally she came back to reality, followed the others and found herself in front of another relic, yet more moving than the first—the veil on which Veronica, in return for her compassion, had found the imprint of the blood-stained face of the Savior.

Rita experienced another harrowing pain, which was soothed this time by the thought of the consolation this simple woman had given to Jesus. Veronica had shown her love in the midst of so many deserters. But the thought of Jesus' face covered with blood haunted Rita. Now that she had "seen," her prayers would take on an added dimension. Once again, the thorn was wounding her to the core of her heart.

The pilgrimage went on, in an ever-increasing crowd. The sisters of Cascia continued their visits to sanctuaries in the course of the following days: the churches of St. John Lateran, St. Mary Major and St. Paul Outside the Walls. There were many fervent Communions and many opportunities for prolonged prayer. But also, what a number of steps, of initiatives, of jostlings, of waits in endless queues! The sun beat down on the dusty city. Rita accepted these drawbacks with courage. She could not tell anymore whether she was warm or hungry, or whether her legs pained her—so much did her fervor get the better of these human concerns. However, she did not forget her sisters, who were not so stoic as she. Even though the trip had toughened them, they showed signs of fatigue, even of exhaustion. She had to take care to space out the outings and the spiritual exercises so they might have a breathing space.

Naturally the nuns from Cascia were anxious to receive the Holy Father's blessing. They had the privilege of attending a papal audience from which they would bring many spiritual graces to all the community in the monastery.

Nor could they leave Rome without admiring the main monuments. The Renaissance period had not yet produced the artistic wonders that would become the aesthetic glory of this city. But, by that very fact, the memory of the first Christians, those of the periods of darkness and persecution, remained intact in their more or less dilapidated sanctuaries. People prayed there as they had in the days of the early Church, in a familiar and spiritual atmosphere.

In the catacombs one breathed the same air breathed by so many faithful of the past who had been forced to hide in order to worship their true God. One could follow the blood-stained paths of those who had been ruthlessly tracked down and brought to the Coliseum. Oh, that tragic arena which had seen men, women and children tortured to death for only one crime, that of loving Jesus! The sister who had been afraid of the animals of the forest on the way to Rome shuddered with horror at the thought of wild beasts unleashed in this arena. All of the sisters united their sufferings, their endeavors, their self-denials, to those of such heroic Christians, now presented as examples to be followed in their devotion.

Among all these people, no one, of course, took notice of

Sister Rita. Nothing would single her out from the crowd. She moved forward with the other pilgrims, interrupted her slow pace, knelt and rose again. She took part in the ceremonies, listened to those who preached, made the sign of the cross and answered the group prayers as everyone else was doing. Only her face, at certain moments, betrayed the intensity of her inner emotions. But who in the course of a pilgrimage would ever take notice of the facial expression of one particular sister within a group from the same religious order?

Perhaps her companions were the only ones to catch, at times, a fleeting glimmer of Rita's deep fervor. They themselves were too taken up by everything they saw and felt, to be much concerned about that. And then, hadn't Rita always been something of a mystic?

Shortly before they were to leave Rome, the sisters of Cascia returned to St. Peter's for a solemn ceremony: the canonization of the Franciscan Bernardine of Siena. There were hymns, lights, a eulogy on the new saint and prominent personalities dressed in splendid attire. Never had the nuns seen anything like this. In the midst of such splendor, Rita's hushed footsteps echoed under the stone vaulting. In all humility, she stood behind a pillar and fervently followed the celebration that already gave a glimpse of paradise.

Never would she have thought that, a few centuries later, the full peal of bells would ring, candles would glow, prayers would be sung and picked up again by thousands of voices—for her. Yes, all that to honor the sister from the mountains of Umbria, who had become St. Rita.

Right then, in a corner of the huge nave, stood only the humble Sister Rita. In spite of all her courage, she was thinking with apprehension of the long distance to be covered before they would reach Cascia again. To her, the St. Mary Magdalen monastery seemed far, so far away.

Chapter 9

Keeping Vigil in the Semi-Darkness

Once again, the sisters prayed and sang as they walked along the roads leading them back to Cascia. But during rest periods, there was no lack of subjects of conversation. These were perhaps too numerous from Rita's point of view, for she, like the Blessed Virgin, would have "treasured all these things and pondered them in her heart" (cf Lk 2:19). However, she could hardly prevent her sisters from sharing their thoughts and impressions with one another.

And then, wherever they stopped, people would question them. Those who had not had the privilege of making this pilgrimage would ask them to give an account, to describe it. The sisters would have lacked charity if they had refused to do so. Light must not remain hidden under a bushel (cf Mt 5:15).

The same happened in Cascia when they finally returned to their monastery. In some way, the graces they had brought back from Rome were shared by the whole community. In those times of difficult traveling, the faithful who returned from the Eternal City were held in admiration. At the beginning of the century, had not Joan of Arc's mother become known as "*Isabelle Romée*" because she had been to Rome? If the expressions used in Umbria were different, the prestige was no less great.

Rita took no notice of this. When the superior ordered her to give an account of the trip to the sisters who had remained behind at St. Mary Magdalen, she related what seemed to be essential. For her, the essential was whatever could be viewed as strictly spiritual. Her listeners, however, were eager to know other details which she willingly would have left out. Happily, the abbess asked additional questions, thus allowing the sisters

63

to imitate her. They did not hesitate to do so.

"Give us a description of St. Peter's Basilica, Sister Rita."

"Were there many foreigners in Rome?"

"Tell us about the Holy Father."

Rita answered as best she could. Then, having said what she had to say, she returned to her dear cell and turned her thoughts to God. She knew very well that at recreation time her traveling companions would be eager to tell about incidents of secondary importance, incidents that had occurred during the trip and during their stay in Rome.

Indeed, one could soon hear words like these coming from the groups:

"... yes, sisters, in the Corno!"

"Providence did watch over us."

"The heat! Unbearable...."

"...all those steps!"

"Unforgetable!"

Sister Rita would go by, seemingly hearing nothing. Since she had seen the relics of the passion, she had increased her penances and prayers. She felt that, until then, she had not really known how to love.

A few days after her return, she noticed that her sisters were again beginning to avoid her. As she touched her forehead, which had never ceased to pain her, she felt that the thorn had reappeared and that a discharge had begun to flow from it again.

The atmosphere around her was again beginning to reek with the terrible stench.

Sister Rita was not surprised. On the contrary, she rejoiced at the thought that her prayers had been answered once more. Her trip to Rome had been much in keeping with the designs of Providence for her. But around her were astonishment and murmuring. Some would assert that she was "not all that holy," since she had been disgraced once more. Others would maintain that this fact meant that the Lord was keeping a close watch on her and had given her a timely respite to make her pilgrimage possible. No one knew the secrets of her dialogues with God, and no one needed to know.

However, the consequences of this situation were the

same as they had been previously. Once again, Rita found herself quarantined. Torn between her regard for this obviously divine favor and her wish to respect the sensitivity of the sisters, the abbess practically subjected her to seclusion. Only one sister would come, in haste, to bring her meals. There was no more question of asking her anything about Rome. The stench was too strong in her little alcove.

Sister Rita could, therefore, devote the major part of her time to prayer and penance. She gave herself to these with a zeal renewed by the memories of her pilgrimage. Never before had she been so vividly aware of the part she could and should take in the passion of Christ. More often than ever, she scourged herself and fasted.

On the other hand, during her trip and her stay in Rome she had come into contact with people of all sorts. Among these, she had noticed or sensed many afflictions, physical as well as moral. How she wished she could help these people! How many people throughout the whole world were in search of eternal salvation.

Therefore, since she felt the circle of isolation tightening around her, she by contrast broadened her prayer to include intentions for the whole world. She would do whatever was in her power to comfort her distant brothers and sisters. Such was the role of the religious—men and women—who spent their lives in monasteries. Sometimes, lay people would say that they were "useless," that they would do better to nurse the sick or teach.

How cruelly unjust! Yes, they did serve—those who presented their sorrows to the Lord for those who were not sorry, their offerings for those who did not offer. Sisters like Rita of Cascia and Thérèse of Lisieux spiritually sustained the work of those laboring in the world to restore order and sow seeds of kindness. While they remained hidden from the world, they intensely irradiated this same world.

At the same time, Sister Rita's contemporaries were not mistaken. In spite of her humility and self-effacement, her reputation for holiness was gradually growing in the city and neighboring regions. People would say that somewhere within the walls of the St. Mary Magdalen monastery, there existed a stigmatist who devoted herself to meditative prayer and penance and who obtained "everything she wanted from the Lord."

Some of the regular beggars who knocked at the door of the monastery had had a glimpse of her, no doubt. And her sisters did not refrain from speaking about her, more or less confidentially, to relatives who came to visit them. People also recalled that, in the past, her admission into the community had been brought about in a very mysterious fashion. Some elderly people had even revived memories of accounts given by their parents concerning the miraculous healing of a harvester while he had been close to a baby surrounded by bees.

To these facts were added the wonders of which people were now speaking. The wound, which had disappeared and reappeared, was only an occasion for the rebirth of the golden legend already growing around Sister Rita. Some believed in it; others did not. But the believers were the greater number. Little by little, people saw not only the sick and needy running up to the St. Mary Magdalen monastery. Persons of all walks of life were coming to beg for favors. They all had the one and same wish: to see Sister Rita, to confide to her their worries, their fears and their hopes, to ask her to pray for them.

But Sister Rita refused to be seen. At first, she was surprised, than a little annoyed by this renown which held no attraction for her. She wanted to remain humbly hidden from the world. Rita had not chosen monastic life to put herself in the limelight. Besides, she would never be able to come near these people. They would flee at the sight of her, at the smell of her wound. And the abbess would never allow it.

Everyone's intentions were simply conveyed to her. To each one, she would forward the answer that she would pray. What she did not say was that she would also deny herself to provide added support to her prayers for those who placed their trust in her.

On one particular morning, in the steep, narrow streets of Cascia, an elderly woman was walking back and forth between her own house and that of her neighbor. A passerby asked her, "Is she all alone?"

"Yes. Her mother asked me to watch over her. She left at dawn, telling no one where she was going. No doubt to see some healer! The poor girl can get so ill at times!"

Through the open door, one could see the adolescent stretched out on her bed. Francesca's wan face was surrounded by neatly braided brown hair. Her large, feverish eyes shone. When she was two, this youngest child of a widow had had a bad fall in their small home. She had never walked since. Now, she would remain there, sadly watching her sisters and her friends run and skip. Sometimes, sharp pains would bring tears to her eyes.

Never had her mother left her for such a long time. Why hadn't she returned? And why, when she had left, had she made her promise to pray very hard?

An hour later, the mother appeared at the end of the street. She was walking at a quick pace. The sight of a crowd gathered in front of her house quickened her heartbeat and, like lightning, sent the wildest thoughts whirling about in her head.

"Something terrible has happened! Francesca, my little one! I shouldn't have left her! And I had such hopes! Perhaps she tried to get up. Perhaps she fell. O holy Virgin, have pity on us!"

But, who was breaking away from the excited group? Who was this girl with rosy cheeks leaping, flying to meet her, throwing herself into her arms?

"Mamma! Mamma! I am healed! You see, I can walk and I can run! Oh, Mamma, come and dance with me!"

With tears and laughter, the mother whisked her off to the church nearby and, from there, to the St. Mary Magdalen monastery while she repeated in her excitement, "Thank you, Lord! And let us go and thank Sister Rita also. I asked her to pray for you this morning. God is good. Long live Sister Rita!"

From the houses along the way, an exuberant crowd emerged. They had heard the news, and so they followed the woman and her daughter to the main entrance of the monastery.

As all of them were knocking together on the door, the sisters, who were quietly having their simple meal, became alarmed. Of course, Sister Rita was not there. Alone in her cell, she was fasting and praying.

When she was told about the miracle just obtained, Rita was both happy and embarrassed. She had a message sent to the visitors, telling them that she shared their joy and would continue to pray for them. Then, she quickly immersed herself again in deep prayer, giving God all the glory for this healing in which she had been but the humble instrument. That same evening, her sisters found her prostrate at the back of the chapel, the wound on her forehead running more than ever. Deep in her heart, Rita was singing a vibrant act of thanksgiving.

From then on, Sister Rita's intercessions were more and more in demand. Several more times she would obtain results which, although less spectacular than the first cure, would be striking enough to spread her reputation throughout the neighborhood.

In the meantime, Rita was caught between her wish for self-effacement and her compassion for others; between physical pain and the delights of the soul; between the regard that the majority had for her and the skepticism expressed by a few. She was becoming weaker, for she was getting on in years. Soon she would be confined to bed.

Intentions for prayers were transmitted to her. Newly-born children and the dying were recommended to her prayers. And there were more difficult cases as well. One evening, for example, the sisters received an urgent request from a man whose wife was possessed by the devil. "Only Sister Rita can deliver her from evil!" he told them.

How many days of prayer, how much fasting, how many mortifications would be needed for Rita to succeed in driving out this relentless enemy? God alone would know!

When, at last, the sufferer had been freed from evil and presented herself at the door of the monastery to express her profuse thanks, Sister Rita was lying on her cot, spent of all her strength almost crushed by the intensity of this fierce struggle. Would she remain in this world much longer?

Chapter 10

Land of Saints

While Sister Rita was drawing graces upon the people around her through her union with Jesus on the cross, there was no lack of other holy people in her country.

Since Signor Bernardone's son had given up everything to become the *Poor Man* of Assisi two centuries before, the seed had grown. For some time, in the various provinces of what would one day become Italy, people had witnessed the blossoming of a true nursery of saints. Some had already been officially recognized as such: for example, Bernardine of Siena, whose canonization the sisters of St. Mary Magdalen had seen in Rome. Others, still alive or already in heaven, would soon be declared saints.

Two Franciscan preachers, still living, were to be canonized one day: John Capistran and James della Marca. The second, especially, was very well known to the people of Cascia. His fiery sermons, preached during an unforgettable Lent, had set the folly of the cross ablaze in Rita's heart.

A short time before Rita was born, Catherine of Siena had died in the peace of the Lord. This humble religious, favored with divine inspirations, has now been officially declared a "Doctor of the Church." Among other graces, she had received the gift of eloquence and was given the task of helping Pope Gregory XI decide to come out of his exile at Avignon and return to the See of Rome. Her good works for the sick and her spirit of self-denial had led her to a bed of pain from which her soul took its flight for the heights of heaven.

Other great mystics, Margaret of Cortona and Angela of Foligno, had walked the way of holiness a short time before Rita had been born.

One of her contemporaries would become St. Frances of Rome. Both had almost identical lives and destinies. Frances, a rich Roman patrician—this was about the only difference between the two—had like Rita, married against her will. She had children, was widowed after many afflictions and ended her days in a cloister.

It was, therefore, not surprising that the Holy Spirit should now take pleasure in blowing over Cascia. It stands to reason that the Italian language will be much spoken in the gardens of paradise.

It was now Sister Rita's turn to prepare herself for the end of her journey on earth. She did not leave her mattress anymore and she hardly ate. As had been the case with Catherine of Siena, the Eucharist eventually became both her bodily food and her spiritual nourishment.

More than ever, from within as well as from outside the monastery, intentions for prayers were entrusted to her. She would offer her sufferings for all who had faith in her intercession. Pale and emaciated, she was tortured with pain, which she concealed the best she could. The only animated part of her were her eyes—her brown eyes shining as much from fervor as from fever. This was the gaze that impressed the few sisters other than the infirmarians who were brave enough to venture into her cell. The thorn was always there and, with it, *the stench*, the terrible stench in addition to the unpleasant smells associated with illness.

Now and then, nevertheless, some woman from the outside world would take the risk of penetrating into this obscure place of seclusion. A relative or friend who had remained loyal to the memories of former days would ask to be admitted to Rita's bedside. By dint of insistence, she would succeed.

One particular morning, Rita was not as feverish as she had been. She was able to say a few words to the priest who brought her Holy Communion. Then, refusing to drink anything nutritious, she bowed her head and joined her hands. One could not tell whether she was praying or sleeping. The one alternated with the other, no doubt.

The awareness of an unusual presence in her room made Rita open her eyes. No, she was not mistaken. There, in the narrow space between the bed and the wall, breathing in the confined air of the room without batting an eyelid, was Catalina, standing still, somewhat embarrassed. This favorite cousin of hers, born like herself in Rocca-Porena, had often come to visit her in the parlor. And yet, Catalina could hardly recognize the sick Rita; her features had altered so much in a few months. The illness had progressed at a frightening pace.

"Rita."

"Catalina, you've come."

The two cousins clasped hands. In spite of all her fondness and compassion for Rita, the visitor could not bring herself to lean over too close to the haggard face that gave off such a stench. Rita understood and, far from blaming her cousin, smiled sweetly. It had been a long time since such light had brightened her eyes.

They did not exchange the trivially deceptive words that are too often spoken in trying circumstances. Rita was little concerned about a possible cure. Besides, she had no illusions about that. She lived only for the offering of herself and in anticipation of her true homeland. On her part, the cousin knew Rita's feelings and sensed that the hour was near.

And so, they were both content to recall the distant past in but a few words. Recovering some strength, Rita would reply to her cousin who whispered softly, "Do you remember?" speaking of the joys of bygone days—festive processions in their little town, beautiful flowers carefully grown by Amata.... Each time, the sick Rita answered with solemn sweetness, "Yes, yes."

However, Rita was not able to carry on a conversation for any length of time. Catalina soon understood that and rose to leave.

"I shall come back, Rita. You rest now. Here, I brought some honey to soothe your throat. And, tell me, what would you like me to bring next time?"

Still impressed by her childhood memories, Rita must not

have been much aware of the reality around her. No doubt, she had not seen the white snowflakes flying about behind the gable window of her cell. It was now midwinter and the January snow had covered Cascia and its neighborhood for several days. Without hesitation, Rita replied, "I would like you to bring me the rose—the one you will find on my rosebush."

Rita was raving, surely. After a brief, friendly nod, Catalina hurried out of the room to search for the infirmarian. She wanted to tell her that Sister Rita was not well, not well at all. It seemed she was delirious.

"Yet, I took care not to tire her, not to prolong my stay."

"This was bound to happen anyway," the sister replied in a reassuring tone. "She is coming to the last phase of her illness. I shall go to see her right away and have Reverend Mother informed."

However, when she reached Rita's bedside, the sister noticed that Rita had resumed her prayer. She appeared neither more nor less feverish than she had previously. In any case, she was perfectly lucid. It must have been a passing bout of fever, no doubt.

Meanwhile, Catalina walked the snow-covered, slippery roads back to Rocca-Porena. Her thoughts were as gloomy as the wintry sky. "Poor Rita! Now she is losing her mind. This business of a rose—to be sure, she thinks it is summertime. How sad to see her come to this!"

When she reached the village, Catalina had to pass by the garden that had belonged to her cousin Rita. The desire to go and have a look came to her. Oh, just to recall the bygone days! A snowbank blocked the path leading to it. Catalina was about to give up. But, suddenly...

A bright spot seemed to beckon to her from the midst of darkened branches and withered thornbushes. Why yes! There was a real rose growing on Rita's rosebush! It was a superb rose with pearly hues, similar to those that blossomed on this bush during the summer months.

With infinite care, Catalina picked the sweet-scented rose that had opened out in the snow. She laid it carefully in a corner of her rustic basket under the light cover. Then, without taking time to rest, she quickly returned to Cascia.

The sisters were astounded when they saw Catalina again on the same day. They were even more amazed when she showed them what she was bringing.

And so, Sister Rita had not been delirious when she asked for this rose, "her" rose. By what gift had she known about the miraculous blossoming? Her cousin took her leave once more, promising to return another day.

Two weeks later, Catalina found Rita weaker and thinner than before, if that could be possible. There was no more question of recalling the past. Catalina stayed only a few minutes. Then, as she set down the preserves she had brought, she asked Rita again, "What would you like to have, the next time I come?"

Rita immediately answered, "The figs that grow on my fig tree!"

Catalina had now learned from experience. When she returned to her village, she went directly to Rita's old orchard. The snow was all gone, but a bitterly cold north wind was blowing from the mountains. The ground was frozen and the fruit trees were hopelessly bare...except... A certain fig tree sported two superb well-ripened figs which were defying the rigors of the season.

When Catalina returned to the monastery, the sisters were almost expecting her, so seriously had they begun to take the apparently incoherent words of the dying Rita. Yes, she was dying, this Rita who, lying on her sickbed, praised the Lord as she joyfully received the miraculous figs.

Nevertheless, in spite of her serious condition, Rita was to linger a few more months. Her life hung by a thread, but her spirit was strong.

One evening, when in the middle of her prayer, she was suddenly surrounded by a strong light. Was it the sun? No. It had set a long time before and the moon had not yet risen.

Drawing herself up slightly, she saw two familiar silhouettes at the door of her cell: Jesus of Nazareth and Mary, his mother.

Rita wanted to rush toward them, but she fell back on her

pillow with a sigh of regret and of yearning. "O my Lord!" she exclaimed. "O Blessed Mother! When will you take me with you at last?"

"Soon," Jesus replied with a smile. "In only three more days!"

And the vision disappeared.

Three more days? Another three days! So thought Rita, who found time even heavier on her hands, now that she had glimpsed the bliss of heaven.

At last it was May 22, 1457. With the first rays of dawn, the window of Rita's cell opened out on a spring in full bloom. But the fragrant and balmy air from outside did not manage to dispel the unpleasant odors that permeated the little room. Gathered around the sickbed were the superior and a few sisters, those who had been able to fit into the room. The others were crowded in the doorway or in the corridors. Sensing that her final hour was drawing near, Sister Rita had requested that the community come to assist her in the reception of the last sacraments.

The group stirred; the nuns moved aside to make way for the chaplain. Having previously heard the dying sister's general confession, he was now bringing her the Bread for travelers on their final journey. He also anointed Rita's emaciated limbs and worn-out face. "...May God forgive you all the evil you have committed with your eyes...your ears...your feet...your hands... your tongue...."

Evil? One might ask whether she had committed any evil at any time, she who used her faculties, both in the world and in the monastery, only to praise God and help her neighbor? But one is never purified enough.

Recollected in her thoughts, her heart at peace, Rita prolonged her act of thanksgiving. Then, regaining some strength for this last time, she asked the abbess to bless her and urged her sisters to be faithful in the observance of the Augustinian rule to its last detail.

"The only way to salvation for us, sisters, is Jesus, the way, the truth, the life...*the life*."

Then, in the Umbrian sky, as the first red rays of dawn appeared, the silvery peal of bells suddenly broke forth. The superior, who had just reverently closed the eyes of the dead sister, glanced at the chaplain. Who had given the order to ring the bells of the monastery and set the full peal of bells in motion as for a feastday? No one, unless the angels from on high were celebrating the entrance of the new elect into eternity!

One sister instinctively tried to open the window wider. All these smells, with the smell of death now added, would become unbearable.

But, much to the contrary, a pleasant scent began to spread in the room while the closed wound on Sister Rita's forehead shone like a star. This miraculous cleansing of the wound, was it not an anticipation of the resurrection?

Chapter 11

Welcomed in Paradise!

Such was the message that the bells were pealing forth, on Rita's part, to the community, to all of Cascia. The shining wound, the permeating fragrance, confirmed this *news bulletin of victory.*

The sisters of the St. Mary Magdalen monastery made no mistake about this. They understood that they now had a new protectress in heaven. To pay their last tribute of respect to Rita, they pressed around the corpse, worn out by a life of penance that had lasted until the age of seventy-six. They dressed Sister Rita in the habit of their order, then moved her to their chapel. There they intended to keep a quiet vigil over her with hearts filled with both sadness and hope. But they had not taken popular enthusiasm into account.

At the sound of the unexpected peal of bells, the people of Cascia had come out into the streets, questioning each other.

"Do you hear? Why are they ringing the bells like this?"

"That comes from the St. Mary Magdalen monastery."

"And yet, this is not a feastday!"

The more inquisitive people hurried to the monastery to find out what was going on. They returned immediately, both moved and excited.

"The bells are ringing for Sister Rita! Sister Rita has just died."

"You must have misunderstood," the neighbors would reply in disbelief. "The knell is what they would toll for a deceased. Rather, the bells must be celebrating her miraculous cure. She has always been so protected."

And the people recalled all over again the miracle of the rose and the miracle of the figs, to mention just the most recent ones. But the messengers were definite. Sister Rita had breathed her last with the first rays of the rising sun. The bells of the monastery had spontaneously begun to ring out in full peal!

After so many wonders, one more or one less, what of it? From that moment, the word "saint" was whispered among the crowd, as it already was whispered in the community. And so, everyone made his or her way to the St. Mary Magdalen monastery. They wanted to see the deceased sister for the last time, and, already, to pray to her rather than pray for her.

The news spread as far as Rocca-Porena. There, it also gave rise to dismay mingled with joy and pride. Relatives and friends of Rita, in their turn, hurried to the monastery.

Among them was a cousin of the Lottis, a rather elderly woman whose right arm had been paralyzed for years. Of an exuberant nature, she was eager to hold her former playmate close to her heart. Not thinking of her handicap, she extended her crippled arm which, to her great surprise, had regained its flexibility and strength and allowed her now to express her fondness for Rita in a warm gesture of affection.

Miraculously healed and beside herself with gratitude, she straightened up and waved both arms about in the middle of the chapel, proving to everyone that, beyond a doubt, she was cured. Meanwhile, she was crying out, "Dearest Rita! Long live St. Rita! Thanks be to God!"

In the meantime, the abbess was in the parlor, having a discussion with the local civil and religious authorities who had come to pay their last respects to the deceased. Three full days had gone by since Rita's soul had departed from her body. Obviously, it was time to make the necessary preparations for the funeral. First, a coffin was needed.

Among the faithful who were forever filing past the body in the chapel, was an ex-carpenter, Cicco Barbaro. He had been forced to discontinue his work as a result of a disabled hand.

"Ah, Sister Rita," he sighed with regret, "if I were still able to exercise my trade, I wouldn't let anyone but myself make a beautiful walnut coffin for you!"

He had hardly finished these words when he felt tingling sensations in his deformed hand. All of a sudden, his hand had become normal again. Master Cicco quickly returned home, grabbed a few boards he had stored away and began to work. His working hands, once again flexible, fashioned a box which became a coffin. Without any difficulty, he himself brought it to the amazed abbess. He was bent on placing Sister Rita's body in the coffin himself. He did so with reverent care, all the while praying and expressing his gratitude in a loud voice. His wife, relatives and neighbors had followed him and now joined in the chorus of his litanies of thanksgiving.

The bells began to toll dolefully for the Requiem Mass, or, rather, for what *should have been* the Requiem Mass. As a matter of fact, one could hardly speak of a funeral ceremony in spite of the ritual tokens of bereavement that surrounded Rita, and still less of a burial.

To begin with, the congregation was torn between grief and proud admiration. To be sure, sobs rose up to the gray vaults. Sister Rita, who would no more be seen, was mourned by everyone. But the hearts of the mourners instinctively felt that she was staying on among her people and watching over them. And, deep down, they experienced a certain delight in sharing the fact that they now had a blessed one in their own country.

Besides, how could they consign her body to the grave, a body which, as the days went by, seemed to be exempt from universal corruption? Although left open, the coffin kept offering for the veneration of the faithful an intact body, a face and joined hands unaltered and free from any unpleasant odor. God was "avenging" this poor sister, who had been cast aside for so long because she was an object of disgust!

Thus, since the dead sister's body had to be shielded from all defilement, it was decided to keep her in the convent chapel and to lay her in state under the altar, near the cross from which she had received the stigmata. Then, in front of Rita, rejected by the grave, a procession began which would never come to an end. People from the city and from the countryside, rich and poor, merged into one and the same prayer, united in trust.

They came to entreat her, to speak to her about their worries and their hopes.

"Sister Rita, heal my child!"

"Sister Rita, convert my husband!"

Who was the first to use the following expression: "You who have *many times overcome the impossible*"? No one knew. But the formula would be revived and adopted by all those who, from age to age, would contribute to making Rita known under this specific invocation: *the saint of the impossible.*

The shrine soon became too small to accommodate the crowd of visitors and pilgrims. Moreover, the peace of the monastery had been somewhat disturbed. It was all very well, even gratifying to see the monastery developing into a privileged center for prayer and processions. On the other hand, what coming and going, what noise, what commotion! The sisters in charge of cleaning were continually sweeping, scrubbing floors, wiping off footprints.

"Oh, these people! Can't they wipe their feet?"

"Look, Reverend Mother, those patches of snow in our chapel!"

"How can we meditate and recite our Divine Office in this continual noise?"

From one generation to the next, the nuns were torn between the honor of having St. Rita's remains in their monastery and the drawbacks stemming from intrusions by visitors.

On their part, the parishioners made demands. They wanted Sister Rita to rest among her people, in the main church of the city where they would be able to come to see her and pray to her in greater numbers.

This came about in 1595. Spontaneous veneration had already lasted for a century and a half. Far from diminishing, it had kept on gathering momentum. After the ceremonies of the translation of her remains had taken place, people developed the habit of organizing great celebrations in honor of Sister Rita. Banners, hymns and public prayers heightened the solemnity of these occasions, especially each May 22, the anniversary of her death.

All these prayers, said by groups or individuals, were

often answered in a spectacular manner. The Lord loved to respond to the prayers of those who asked his help through her who had been his spouse at the foot of the cross. Miracles were performed, either near Rita's tomb or at the touch of her clothes or of objects which had belonged to her. The news of this spread by word of mouth.

At this time, many people could neither read nor write. But a few could paint—among them some of Rita's sisters. On the very day following her death, an anonymous painter had chosen to honor Rita by beginning to illustrate the story of her life. Six paintings, preserved for a long time in the monastery, pictured outstanding episodes.

The first painting showed Rita as a baby in the middle of a harmless swarm of bees, smiling at the angels and at the bees. The second painting showed her following her three protector saints as they led her within the precincts of the St. Mary Magdalen monastery in spite of its walls and bolted doors. The third reproduced her solemn profession. Her countenance was one of submission and triumph as she was receiving the long-desired religious habit of the professed sister from the abbess. The fourth tableau showed her kneeling at the feet of Jesus on the cross while a thorn lodged itself in her serene forehead. The fifth one portrayed her death as she was surrounded by the kneeling community. Finally, the sixth painting pictured her triumphant funeral among the people of Cascia.

Unfortunately, the paintings gradually deteriorated. Others replaced them and were hung on the walls of the St. Mary Magdalen monastery to inform future generations about the life of Rita.

Let us go back to the sixteenth century. The celebrations which were then spontaneously organized to honor St. Rita's relics had sprung solely from popular devotion. But the official Church, that of Rome, had not yet been consulted.

It often happened in those days that, depending on the people around them, simple folk who had died "in a spirit of holiness" would become the objects of excessive veneration.

Nevertheless, Sister Rita's case stands out. Startling incidents, whether recognized as supernatural or not, had occurred immediately after her death. Eleven miracles had already been reported in the first days after she had died. Healings, conversions and various other graces had been received in answer to the requests of those who had prayed to her. Certain wonders had taken place for which no specific request had been made. An example of this was Rita's cousin's recovery of the use of her arm.

The accounts of these wonders were transmitted from one generation to the next, confirmed by the testimonies of painters and of notaries who officially authenticated important or unusual incidents.

This explains why, until the beginning of the seventeenth century, people continued to venerate Sister Rita with more and more solemnity, showing no concern about knowing whether or not such veneration was approved by Rome.

But then things began to change. In 1623, Urban VIII became Pope. His first task was to examine the cases of the "saints," more or less authentic, who abounded in the four corners of the Christian world. It was a matter of sorting out the true from the false, of separating fact from legend, piety from superstition. The new Pope wanted to develope a rigorous new official procedure, so as to put an end to abuses as well as to identify the true cases of holiness.

Would Sister Rita find favor in the eyes of this meticulous Pontiff?

Chapter 12

The Pope in Cascia

With a sigh of relief, Urban VIII left his study, where he had been working out the last details of a delicate case. For two years, he had been vigorously engaged in examining the cases of so many supposed "saints," generally found among the people, who had become the objects of a more or less justified veneration. In Italy, especially, with the local clergy's approval, people had bestowed so many halos without rhyme or reason! Many of the faithful and their clergy, impressed by the example of their great forerunners, saw new "Francises of Assisi" or "Catherines of Siena" everywhere. Legends and fables sometimes interfered and offered as examples people whose lives left much to be questioned. The Pope and his collaborators would need time, calm, quiet, thought and sheer hard work to bring these meticulous investigations to a successful conclusion. Then they would see whether or not there were grounds to begin the proceedings for beatification.

At this moment, Urban VIII had been summoned by another of the duties inherent to his position. These relentlessly morseled his time. His personal work was finished for the day; the hour for papal audiences had rung.

He passed into the great hall set aside for this purpose and asked for the first person to be brought in. His face lit up when he read her name.

This woman was Constance Barberini. Until his recent election Urban VIII had gone by the name of Matteo Barberini. This was his niece, who certainly could have presented herself to him without going through the formal channels of protocol.

But, from now on, this fervent Christian woman refused to see anyone else but the Vicar of Jesus Christ in her uncle. All the more so this morning.

After the official and customary marks of respect, Constance was asked to present her request with all the simplicity expected of relatives. She began in a respectful but resolute tone of voice.

"Most Holy Father—pardon me; I mean, my good Uncle— I know that you are particularly interested in cases apt to be considered for beatification."

"What cause, more or less worthy, does she intend to support?" the Pope asked himself. Without showing his feelings, he motioned her to go on.

"Uncle, some years ago I read some accounts concerning a certain Sister Rita who died in 1457 and whose virtues...."

A kind but skeptical smile dampened Signora Barberini's enthusiasm. Somewhat taken aback but still persistent, she resumed her point after a slight hesitation.

"Oh, I know very well, Uncle, that you advise people to be extremely cautious with regard to these popular judgments, which are a little hasty sometimes. But Church authorities in high positions have heard about Sister Rita and the miracles attributed to her. She appears to justify the trust people have had in her for a century and a half. Your steward-secretary, Monsignor Fauste Poli himself, has told me much on this subject."

Urban VIII, who until then had lent half an ear to his niece's arguments, began to listen more attentively. If his steward himself was interested in this, the rumor needed to be closely examined.

"And who was this Sister Rita?"

"A sister in the St. Mary Magdalen monastery in Cascia in the diocese of Spoleto, your former diocese, Uncle." Constance's voice betrayed some anxiety but was also filled with hope.

The Holy Father pondered and drew upon his memories. Cascia? Cascia? It was a small city lost in the mountains. He had visited it once. Yes, he remembered now. In that country which is poor and harsh, people must lead austere lives, with no fear of self-denial.

But this Sister Rita? Actually, he had heard people speak

about her during his brief stay there. "The sister of the thorn," they called her in that area. Miracles were attributed to her, perhaps neither more nor fewer than to many others. Pressed for time, the then bishop had not been able to visit her tomb as he had urgently been asked to do. A tomb or a reliquary? Someone had mentioned a sarcophagus, and also—he remembered now—the preservation of her body. Or had it been embalmed?

Urban VIII was now keenly interested. He asked his niece to come back some other day with Canon Poli for a longer visit to tell him the story of this religious of Umbria. He himself would immediately order an inquiry on site.

After a last curtsy, Constance Barberini withdrew, pleased with the effect her intervention had had on her uncle. And the next visitor was ushered in.

The inquiry carried out by the commission appointed by the Pope lasted two long years. It had become obvious that the case was worth looking into. A delegation from Rome, presided over by Monsignor Pietro Colangeli, first went to Cascia. In the presence of medical and legal experts, the delegation ascertained the inexplicable preservation of her body, after more than one hundred and sixty years. The officials inhaled the sweet fragrance which emanated from it. They examined testimonies certified in the presence of notaries of the wonders connected with Sister Rita. They studied older accounts describing facts of a similar nature, not to mention the revelations discreetly whispered by those who claimed they had obtained spiritual graces through prayers made in front of this altar.

For these reasons, in 1628, after having called upon the Holy Spirit, the Pope signed the decree of beatification.

The ceremonies took place in Cascia on May 22, anniversary of Sister Rita's "birth in heaven." Among the many spectators, many were indebted to her for favors, both material and spiritual. Others were descendants of the first persons to have been miraculously healed. Others numbered some of Rita's relatives or neighbors among their ancestors. For the glory of the newly blessed, they eagerly collected accounts passed on from generation to generation. A great honor was reflected upon the city, upon the whole region. First and foremost in the assembly, along with the leading citizens of Cascia, were the present sisters of the St. Mary Magdalen monastery led by their abbess, Sister Lucia Cittadoni. Inhabitants of Rocca-Porena also were there, each claiming a more or less distant kinship with the Lottis or the Mancinis of the 1400's.

The reliquary occupied a place of honor in the middle of the sanctuary. After the entrance hymns and other hymns and prayers, the pontifical decree was read. It declared blessed this Rita Lotti, a religious, who had died in a spirit of holiness in 1457. Then began a long sermon, a form of eulogy.

The crowd was very much taken up at first, but then began to be restless. The weather in Cascia was very warm in May, especially in this overcrowded church. The ventilation through its open doors did not manage to cool it to any degree. At first, murmurs were heard, then loud exclamations.

"Don't push, I say!"

"I want to see!"

"So do I. She healed my father!"

"I'm a distant cousin of hers...."

"That's what you say!"

"Through marriage, in any case!"

"And then?.... But don't push."

People became agitated. One was supporting his wife, another was helping his brother jostle his neighbors. In spite of the sacred character of the place and the solemnity of the moment, there was a stir in the crowd which risked degenerating into a brawl. Suddenly, the whole congregation was visibly startled, and silence abruptly fell on the crowd. The preacher stopped praising Sister Rita's merits while the faithful near the coffin pointed to it with a gesture of terror. People whispered from row to row.

"She moved...."

"Blessed Rita is displeased with us!"

In fact, the members of the clergy present in the sanctuary, the leading citizens, the sisters, all had been able to ascertain this incredible phenomenon. The eyes in the face that had been still for so many years had suddenly opened at the sound of the irreverent commotion. They had cast a stern look toward the aisle of the church where the guilty ones were to be found. Calm was immediately restored. Here was another wonder which would be taken into consideration at the time of the canonization proceedings.

However, these proceedings would not be undertaken right away. Too many events, most of them tragic, would shake the world in the years and centuries to come. Wars, revolutions and other changes would disturb minds, arouse passions and absorb attention in general.

At last, the twentieth century dawned. Leo XIII now sat on St. Peter's throne. One day Thérèse Martin would ask him to allow her to enter the Carmel at Lisieux at age fifteen. With wisdom and prudence; he would advise her simply to act according to the decisions of her spiritual directors.

Leo XIII had heard about the miracles Sister Rita had been credited with since her beatification. Among others, there had been movements of her body similar to the one that occurred on the day of her beatification. He had read and meditated everything about Blessed Rita. But like his distant predecessor Urban VIII, he also wished to take all the necessary precautions before yielding to the wishes of those asking him to take the steps preparatory to canonization. Results of inquiries, verifications of facts, proofs and counter-proofs followed one upon the other in the Vatican. At last they began the proceedings properly so-called, during which the devil's advocate with his arguments "*against*" confronted the defense advocate championing arguments "*in favor*" of the canonization.

A sense of honesty on the part of the Church forces it to weigh scrupulously all the elements of its judgment.

In Rita's case, the decision came in 1900. On May 24, the feast of the Pentecost, Leo XIII proclaimed that the religious sister of Cascia would henceforth be venerated under the name of St. Rita. May 22 would remain her feastday.

All the bells of St. Peter's rang out in full peal! The renovated basilica had long since been crowned with its cupola. The Eternal City had taken on a new look since the Middle Ages. The Renaissance, the movement for the unification of Italy, and modern times had all left their marks.

How different Rome was from the city admired by a group of nuns who had walked from the mountains of Umbria to attend the Jubilee of 1450! In 1900, pilgrims made their way to the sanctuary in horse-drawn buses or carriages. A few were even driving those queer horseless vehicles that were ushering in what would become the century of the automobile. But hearts remained the same. There, in former times, had stood the humble Rita in the shadow of a pillar, attending the canonization of St. Bernardine of Siena. On this same spot today proudly stood other people from her country, filled with wonder and fervor as she had been then. There were also Catholics from all over Italy and representatives of the whole world.

The hidden rose of Rocca-Porena, the sister who had been relegated to her austere cell so as not to inconvenience her companions, was now receiving homage from all the world. The Lord whose suffering she had willingly shared now publicly revealed that he was giving her a share in his glory.

The altar was ablaze with glittering gold and garlands of dazzling lights. The Holy Father came forward, accompanied by the highest dignitaries of the Church. After the reading of the canonization decree, hymns of praise and thanksgiving burst forth. Then followed the unparalleled strains of the most famous choirs, the soaring peals of the grand organ accompanying jubilant hymns of joy, the full peals of bells challenging the skies of Rome. Nothing was too fine to honor this woman who had always lived in seclusion, serving God and neighbor.

Thousands of voices rose in the elated basilica. Millions of voices throughout the world were repeating and will repeat until the end of time the invocation of trust which often becomes a last resort for help: *St. Rita of Cascia, pray for us!*

In the Footsteps of St. Rita

In Cascia

Should it ever be possible for you to go to Cascia, you will immediately be immersed in the atmosphere and the setting that St. Rita knew. Of course, living conditions have changed since her day and certain material aspects of the environment as well. But the essentials remain.

You will see the city terraced up the mountainside and dominated by the spires of its churches. The present city spreads both above and below the city of old. Over the years, people have built here, cleared the grounds there, and rebuilt farther on. The weathering effects of time, and those of the earthquakes as well, have altered the setting to some extent.

Yet, close by the homes, beside monuments of recent origin, you will still be able to admire picturesque spots that have lost nothing of their charm: ivy-clad walls, ruins of towers and even remains of Roman constructions.

You will naturally direct your steps first to the basilica-shrine which treasures St. Rita's body. This building dates from 1947. The fervor of our times has raised this edifice, more vast and modern than the old one of 1707. We enter it through a street bordered with arches. The white facade, framed by two pinnacle turrets, speaks of peace and simplicity. The cross forms the armature of the stained-glass window rising above the entrance, as it also formed the framework of Sister Rita's piety. We find it again on the pediment of the sanctuary.

By way of compensation, the interior is sumptuously embellished with works of great contemporary artists—a Way of the Cross in marble, frescoes, marvelous paintings. In the left apse, we have the chapel of Saint Rita. Here, so as to render homage to her, popular devotion has called upon all the riches of this world. Nothing is too beautiful for this woman who was always seeking to be last. The Gospel says: "Whoever lowers himself, shall be raised" (cf Lk 18:14). Behind a screen, the silver reliquary rests on a sculptured marble pedestal, and the supporting pillars are of crystal interwoven with gold.

But you will experience a strange feeling as you contemplate the most precious of the jewels displayed there: St. Rita's body, exactly as it was when her soul left it to fly up to heaven. The face, still intact, only a little darkened by time, has preserved its expression of profound peace. The garments are those of the Order of St. Augustine of her time, and a white veil covers her head.

Facing this chapel, in the right apse, you will be able to see another chaple dedicated to Our Lady of Consolation. Frescoes illustrating various episodes in the life of Mary beautify it. Under the altar, a silver urn preserves the relics of Blessed Simon Fidati, another native of Cascia. There again, outstanding artists have worked for the glory of God and of those who have been faithful in their love of him.

You will find other traces of St. Rita in the collegiate church of St. Mary. Still to be seen is the stone basin from which water for her baptism was drawn. How can you not help imagining baby Rita smiling in the arms of her godmother, in the presence of the moved and recollected family? Just think! The miraculous child was then starting on her Christian journey. God alone knew then that he would lead her to the summits.

Later, it was in this same church that she, a religious among the others and already middle-aged, had come one Lenten evening. The sermon made such an impression on her that her whole spirituality took on a new meaning.

As you come out of the church and are about to follow the path climbing to the monastery, you will recall Sister Rita, who leaned on a rough-hewn walking stick, painfully following her companions as she stumbled over the stones. Her heart was still filled with the sorrowful mysteries she had just meditated; her body was weary from having walked in the procession of the cross. Nevertheless, she found that nothing was too harsh when she united herself to the tragic climb of Calvary.

You will see the monastery, a large plain structure, spread out on the top of the hill and looking out toward the world through its many windows. It had more modest proportions in the days of St. Rita, whose name has succeeded that of St. Mary Magdalen.

An earthquake damaged this structure at the beginning of the eighteenth century. Thanks to King John V of Portugal, it was then repaired and even enlarged. Thanks especially to St. Rita, by whose intercession the king was healed and inspired to make a generous donation as a token of gratitude. Thus, the left wing was built.

As you wander through this monastery, you will sense Sister Rita going by—she who so often prayed and worked on these premises.

In this choir, early one morning, she was found by the community, even though the doors of the monastery were all bolted. Here, she attended many religious services. She hurried down these corridors on her way to perform some work of charity or to go to prayer. She went about her various tasks, willingly keeping the most unpleasant ones for herself. Within these walls, she dreamed of making a pilgrimage to Rome; it was here that she prayed for and was granted a temporary healing so she could go.

She returned to these premises, her eyes and heart filled with the wonders of the Eternal City. She was happy she had earned the merits attached to the Jubilee and had seen the Holy Father. And, of course, she was relieved that she had managed to bring the little flock entrusted to her care safely back home to the monastery in spite of the many hazards encountered during the trip.

Then, these gloomy walls once more closed in around her. And, silently, she resumed her labors and sufferings, her eyes forever fixed on Christ, the victim.

You will be allowed to visit her cell, narrow and stifling— the cell where she made her meditative prayer and practiced harsh austerities. If these grim walls could speak, they would have much to tell, rather more about prolonged prayers and scourgings than about rest. Rest! Sister Rita took so little of it, on a pallet whose replica can still be seen in a corner.

This room has now been transformed into a chapel. There, Rita lived the last years of her life as a recluse, those years when her repulsive wound excluded her from the community. There, she felt the vitality ebb out of her emaciated body in the course of her terminal illness. There, she received from her kinswoman the gifts that had miraculously flourished in the snow—the rose in January, the ripened figs.

It was into this denuded alcove that, somehow or other, her sisters crowded to attend Rita in her last moments, while a joyous peal of bells acclaimed her entrance into paradise. And it was there that the stench exuding from her wound was replaced by a sweet fragrance emanating from her undefiled body, spreading throughout the room.

In this monastery, you will also see the series of coffins that have successively been used for the saint. Thus, you will be able to gauge the growth of the people's veneration for her. Initiated at the very moment of her death, this veneration assumed dimensions that constantly grew in scope throughout the years. The series of investigations and the transfers into sarcophagi that were progressively more and more ornate are a moving testimony of the growth of this devotion.

First, here is the *Cassa Umile*, a modest wooden box in which a nun's remains were ordinarily placed. For Sister Rita, that coffin was the one the disabled carpenter Cicco suddenly found himself able to make despite his deformed hands. He who deplored so much the fact that he could not pay his last respects to Sister Rita with his work, took great pains in fulfilling this task properly.

But the fruit of his labor was used for only ten years. This coffin had been destined to bear the deceased sister in her grave. But since the earth rejected Sister Rita, how could this intact body be kept in this coffin? Ten years later, at the time of a first official acknowledgment, it was decided to lay her in state in a more sumptuous sarcophagus—the *Cassa Solenne*.

This one is adorned with paintings representing Rita both alone and in the company of Mary Magdalen, near Christ at the tomb. Near her head, traces of an epitaph could be seen until 1745. Written in the dialect used in Rita's days, this inscription told of her merits and also implored her protection. This was a custom commonly observed in the Middle Ages for those whom people wished to honor after their death.

In 1745 there was a new transfer. The coffin used at this time is still preserved in another room in the convent. It is displayed with the professed sister's ring, with the saint's rosary and with a mantle that belonged to her. These relics stir the hearts of visitors who reverently contemplate them. All this appears both immediate and remote at the same time!

Finally, in 1930, the body was placed in the present silver reliquary. The previous coffin was then placed among the other relics.

You can also collect your thoughts at the feet of the Christ from whom Sister Rita, upon her insistent request, received the thorn. This thorn came and lodged itself in her forehead after she returned from the unforgettable Lenten sermon.

When Sister Rita died, six paintings were hung on the walls of the monastery by her contemporaries. These paintings, the aim of which was to perpetuate the memory of the main events of her life, were probably the work of one of her sisters. As mentioned earlier in this book they do not exist anymore. But others, beyond doubt inspired by these first perishable paintings, have taken their place. From these can be grasped a general idea of the saint's physical appearance, of her sisters' features, of the abbess's attitudes, of the clothes and religious accessories worn at the time.

Many people hurried past the threshold of the entrance door on their way to beg Sister Rita for some bread, for health care or for hope and comfort. Her smile soothed equally the rich and the poor; her prayer surrounded them with the same concern.

Along these sloping streets wound the funeral procession to which the walls and the worn-out stone pavements still bear witness today.

If you happen to be in Cascia on May 22, you will be able to take part in the solemn procession which highlights the feast of St. Rita every year.

Without waiting for this day, be sure to take a stroll in the monastery gardens. A superb vinestock, spread out over the wall of the cloister, will draw your attention. It stretches its protective arms across the sunlit facade and, in season, gloriously displays mellow clusters of grapes. Could anyone believe that the origin of this thriving and productive vine was a tiny stick of dry wood? As a novice, without understanding why her superior was ordering her to do so, Rita watered it for months. She thought she was only performing her duty of obedience, doing an exercise aimed at molding her character. One fine day, the sap sprang up in an unexpected manner, aptly symbolizing the grace brought about through prayer and humility. In this, St. Rita began to show that she could obtain the impossible from God through perseverance and a submissive attitude to his will.

The miraculous rosebush of Rocca-Porena was transplanted into these very gardens. It sank roots in such a way that fragrant bushes now bloom every spring and fascinate both the sisters and visitors.

Finally, as soon as Sister Rita's soul took its flight, bees, in exchange, came to Cascia. They are still there: a species of bees which disappeared from everywhere else a long time ago. At the monastery, they have remained as they were in the Middle Ages—black with a touch of red: a mysterious message from the "Saint of the bees."

There are other "bees" in Cascia. They are the girls of an orphanage built in the vicinity of the sanctuary by the "work" which keeps the memory and the devotion to St. Rita alive. They are called "St. Rita's Little Bees." Watch them playing on the playground. This orphanage is nothing like the gloomy image that the term could conjure up. Here, the girls are happy and outgoing, very comfortable, close to their protectress. The resources of this institution are largely drawn from the sale of the bulletin called *From Bees to Roses*. This bulletin is distributed locally and in the main pilgrimage centers. One can also subscribe to it by mail. St. Rita blesses in a special way those who take interest in the girls welcomed in her name.

Then, you will follow the roads leading you through the countryside and up the mountains to Rocca-Porena. There, as you trace the course of Rita's life back in time, you will gradually understand how this soul, which, after many detours, was to enter the cloister to which she so ardently aspired, was hammered into shape by the joys and sorrows of this world.

At Rocca-Porena

These roads, of course, bear no resemblance to the sharp slopes and poorly kept paths of the fifteenth century. Now there are roads suitable for modern transportation. But the landscape is still what it was then: a simple village tucked away in a hollow in an awe-inspiring landscape of rugged and majestic mountains. The breezes are laden with the scents of wild plants; the sky is now serene, now tormented. With a little imagination, the kind that is stirred in the heart, you will easily picture the Rocca-Porena where little Rita was born and grew up.

It is she who will first come out and meet you when you approach the Corno mountain stream. You will be forced to recall that nocturnal scene when a brave woman all in tears came there by torchlight to identify her husband's bloodstained body. The howling storm, the ominous shadows constantly distorted by the movements of the flame—all that will appear tragically real to you.

Going back still further in time, you will reach the village where other aspects of the saint will take your mind away from this dismal scene. She who will come out to meet you will be the young woman, in turn unhappy, then serene, the mother holding a baby's hand in each of her own. You will see the young woman eager to attend to her aged parents' needs, hiding her anguish when forced to become a fiancée. Under this sky, before this nature which speaks of the Creator, Rita very often prayed silently as she came and went, fulfilling her daily duties.

Then, the silhouette of the little girl, at the same time laughing and recollected, will pass by, followed by the tiny silhouette of the baby being taken to the city to be baptized.

Antonio Lotti, Amata, Paul de Ferdinand and the twins

will people the streets for you as you mentally reconstruct these scenes.

To give concrete form to these memories, you will visit in turn the various places that witnessed the life of St. Rita or extol her merits.

You will first visit her home, which was transformed into a chapel in 1629, the year following her beatification. The exterior of it is plain—a small structure with bare walls, dominated by a bell-tower of comparable proportions. A rounded porch with a low gate gives access to the interior of the house.

Inside, there is a vaulted sanctuary decorated with frescoes of angels and from which hang ornamental lamps. Above the altar, a large painting shows Rita receiving the thorn.

Thorns—did she not have to cope with some at the very beginning of her married life? The remains of her home, enshrined within the chapel, remind us that she experienced here her joys and sorrows as wife and mother. Long before yours, her prayer of thanksgiving or of entreaty, but always in conformity with God's plan, rose up from these premises to the Father.

Tradition does not mention Rita's paternal home. It was likely destroyed by an earthquake. Chroniclers say it stood some hundred steps away from the de Ferdinand home.

You will also be able to visit the lazaretto—a place which would now be called a dispensary—where Rita came with her usual devotion to nurse the homeless sick. This building has kept its medieval style. Very austere in appearance, it houses a few paintings, notably a fresco of the Annunciation and a bust of St. Rita. All this is subsequent to her times.

Rocca-Porena owed it to itself to erect a sanctuary worthy of the most prestigious and at the same time, the humblest of its children. You will now explore this building.

A modern edifice, it was opened for public worship in 1946. This structure with its white facade rises in a particularly well-chosen setting of green vegetation. We have access to it through a wide flight of steps which opens onto a small esplanade surrounded with arches. You will be welcomed by a statue of St. Rita, dressed as a peasant woman with her arms raised in gesture of prayer.

Inside, you will find paintings, mosaics and stained-glass windows showing Christ on the cross, Our Lady of Sorrows and Sister Rita among her favorite saints: St. Augustine, St. James della Marca, St. John the Baptist, and St. Nicholas of Tolentino. Of course, you will also see the scene of the thorn. Relics of the saint, exposed in a silver custodial, are also venerated there.

Every year crowds of faithful gather in the sanctuary to attend the ceremony of the Blessing of the Roses, an important local feastday celebrated in memory of the miracle of olden days. This practice is also observed in all other centers of prayer dedicated to St. Rita.

Right beside this sanctuary rises the bell-tower of the parish church, St. Montand. This church is the very one St. Rita knew and faithfully attended until the time she entered the monastery. Under these vaults, she murmured prayers Amata had taught her. As she grew up, she entrusted her vocation, her hopes and her fears to the Lord here. The exception was Rita's baptism which, for the lack of a baptismal font, took place in Cascia. All the other family ceremonies of the Lottis and Mancinis took place within this church.

It will seem to you that you can see the nuptial procession led by Paul de Ferdinand appear in the doorway. He is accompanied by his new bride who, while her heart is filled with apprehension, is acclaimed by her neighbors and friends, crowded in the sun-drenched square in front of the church.

In the half-light of the interior, you will recall the coffins of Amata and Antonio, brought into this sanctuary within a short interval to receive the last blessing while their daughter silently wept at one side of the nave.

Sobs, more heartrending yet, mark the funeral ceremony for the treacherously assassinated Paul. Mastering her grief, Rita rises to the occasion and responds to the prayers referring to judgment and hope. She knows that, partly thanks to her, the soul of her now-beloved husband can face its Lord as a true member of the faithful. But, from time to time, she leans over to one or the other of her sons, who stand on each side of her with clenched fists and resolute expression. A word she refuses to accept—vengeance—hovers in the air around her.

Then, another funeral scene. This time, it centers on the remains of these same young men who, one after the other, come here on their final journey. Rita, the sorrowful mother, feels a certain peace stealing within her in the midst of her grief. Her sons died as Christians, their hate having been transformed into forgiveness.

But look around you and come back to our present times. This church is not very large. It preserves its primitive style: romanesque vaulting, stone pavement, wooden pews. It was only during the sixteenth century that it was decorated with paintings: the crowning of the Blessed Virgin and pictures of saints. Among them we find Rita, a Rita already crowned with the halo of holiness at a time when there was not even a thought of her beatification. Here again, popular devotion had anticipated official decrees by many years.

Perhaps in memory of the two adolescents whom Rita, all by herself, managed to bring up so well, Rocca-Porena is the site of an orphanage for boys. This too, is managed by the *Work*. It makes a pair with the *Beehive* of the little Bees of Cascia, as much in the educators' care as in the donors' generosity.

A large structure, well-lighted and comfortable, dominates the center of a garden. Sportsgrounds, training workshops—nothing is lacking in what may contribute to the formation of men, laborers and Christians. As in the case of the girls, happiness lights up the faces of these young people who are living in a willingly accepted and understood discipline. These two educational centers are an extension of St. Rita's work, perpetuated by our prayer and support.

At the far end of the village is St. Rita's garden. It extends to the foothills of the mountains. From there, a tiny valley comes into view and beyond that, paths climb up amid the green vegetation of the opposite slope. Here, the hand of man has domesticated nature, its plants and rocks, all the while treating it with respect. This is a thankless task to which there is no end. You will have no difficulty imagining Rita wandering along these lanes, weeding here, watering there, delicately picking a flower or a fruit.

Rita? At the turn of one of the lanes, you will really meet her under a tree held up by a knotty trunk. But her appearance might be somewhat disconcerting to you, even though the symbol it represents is absolutely logical. A modern sculptor has set up on this spot a bronze sculpture showing Rita on her deathbed being visited by her cousin. This cousin, tenderly bending over Rita, is offering her the miraculous rose which has blossomed out on this very spot in the January snow.

The serene expression on the face of the dying Rita and the loving and awed attitude of the visitor make this a real and stirring scene. The sister, a recluse for so long in her narrow cell, is preparing herself to enter a garden of infinite splendor—that of paradise.

If you have the courage to do so, you will climb the rock—a rather threatening mass—which overlooks Rocca-Porena. The path, rough and tortuous, is marked by the stations of the Way of the Cross.

A small shrine, flanked by two rows of arches, gives a human touch to this impressive summit. Inside, you will admire more particularly a painting showing the saint climbing up to heaven. But you will especially notice a boulder, reverently kept, on which she would kneel when she went up there to pray under the stars or facing the valley.

Following her example, you will be able to collect your thoughts for a moment on this windswept esplanade. You may think you see the poor widow who on a stormy night climbed up these sharp slopes and saw the ground suddenly open up at her feet. This was the final test aimed at probing the depth of her trust after so many changes, delays and rejections, all blocking the way to her vocation.

At last, God was waiting for her at the end of the road in the community to which she was truly destined.

In the evening, you will see an illuminated cross shining in the center of the village. Visible from afar, this cross is a signal and reminder that great things have taken place at Rocca-Porena, things that did not necessarily draw attention at the moment but blossomed forth later in holiness and graces.

Such was the hidden life of the little girl born here almost six hundred years ago, in the home of Antonio and Amata, the *peacemakers*.

Because she followed the cross, Rita is now in full light and endowed with a marvelous power that she uses in favor of those who have succeeded her on earth.

In our difficult and uncertain times, how often we have wished that this notion of peace might become something other than an abstract formula. Rita and her parents show us how, little by little, it is possible to establish peace in a disturbed world. It was no easier for them to obtain it in their times than it is for us in ours. They labored for it according to their means in their humble state of life.

Let us pray to the *saint of the impossible* to inspire us with the same concern. May she obtain divine help for us, so that one day, in spite of the storms, all people of good will may join hands, united in the same love.

Appendix II

Prayers to St. Rita

Prayer for Difficult and Desperate Cases

O glorious and powerful St. Rita, look upon me, a soul in distress prostrate at your feet, who, in my need, turn to you with the sweet assurance of being answered.

In spite of my unworthiness and my lack of fidelity in the past, I hope that my prayers will bend the heart of God. Still, I feel the need of a powerful mediatrix, and you are the one I have chosen, St. Rita, because you hold the incomparable title of *saint of the impossible and desperate cases.*

O dear St. Rita, please take my request to heart. Intercede with God to grant me the grace I need so much and ardently hope to receive *(express the grace you desire).*

Do not let me leave you with my prayer unanswered. If there is any obstacle in me which might prevent my receiving the grace I am asking, help me remove it. Clothe my prayer with your precious merits and offer it to your spouse in heaven in union with yours. Thus, presented by you, his spouse, faithful among the most faithful, you who have shared the sufferings of his passion, how can my prayer then be rejected or remain unanswered?

I place all my trust in you and, through your mediation, I anticipate, with peace in my heart, the fulfillment of my wishes.

O dear St. Rita, do not let me down in my trust and my hope in you, but see that my request be not made in vain. Obtain from God what I am asking of you. Then, I will make known to everyone the kindness of your heart and the all-powerful character of your intercession.

And you, adorable heart of Jesus, who have always proved yourself to be so sensitive to the least of human miseries, allow yourself to be moved by my needs. In spite of my weakness and unworthiness, grant me the grace which is so dear to me and which your faithful spouse, St. Rita, is asking from you for me and with me.

In return for St. Rita's fidelity in always responding to divine grace, for all the gifts you gave her soul in abundance, for all she suffered as a wife and mother and in sharing your harrowing passion, and, lastly, for the extraordinary power of intercession by which you have wished to reward her fidelity—grant this grace so necessary to me.

And you, Blessed Virgin Mary, our kind mother in heaven, depository of divine treasures and dispenser of all graces, strengthen by your powerful intercession the prayer of your great friend, St. Rita, so that God may grant me the favor I am asking. Amen.

Prayer of Thanksgiving

With a deeply moved and grateful heart, I come to you today, glorious and powerful St. Rita.

At the hour of danger, at the time when my happiness and that of those dear to me was threatened, when my soul was afflicted and full of apprehension, I implored you. I begged you, whom everyone calls the *saint of the impossible,* the *advocate of hopeless cases,* the *refuge at the final hour!* I was never disappointed for having placed my trust in you.

I come again to you now, no longer in tears of suffering, but with joy and serenity in my heart, to express my gratitude to you.

This joy, this serenity, I owe to you, dear St. Rita, for having pleaded with God for me in spite of my unworthiness and for having obtained for me the grace I wanted.

I would like to express more appropriately to you the profound feelings of gratitude which fill my heart, holy miracle-worker and comforter of the afflicted, but the very confusion arising from the happiness of having obtained this grace inhibits my power of expressing it adequately and I can only murmur, thank you, St. Rita.

To prove my gratitude to you in a more realistic manner, I promise that, with an ever-increasing zeal, I will make your devotion more widely known. I will make you loved by those to whom your name is yet unknown and who do not have, as I do, the good fortune of having experienced your infinite kindness.

Insofar as this will be possible for me, I promise to help foster your devotion and to attend the ceremonies celebrated in your honor.

I resolve, from this day on, to fulfill my duties as a Christian with a greater sense of commitment and fervor.

O dear St. Rita, I ask you to offer my sincere resolutions to God and thank him in my name for the grace generously given to me.

Finally, may you never abandon me and continue to let me enjoy your holy and active protection, so that after having benefited from it in this life, I may one day find you again in heaven and express in better ways my gratitude to you. Amen.

St. Paul Book & Media Centers

ALASKA
750 West 5th Ave., Anchorage, AK 99501 907-272-8183.

CALIFORNIA
3908 Sepulveda Blvd., Culver City, CA 90230 310-397-8676.
1570 Fifth Ave. (at Cedar Street), San Diego, CA 92101 619-232-1442;
   619-232-1443.
46 Geary Street, San Francisco, CA 94108 415-781-5180.

FLORIDA
145 S.W. 107th Ave., Miami, FL 33174 305-559-6715; 305-559-6716.

HAWAII
1143 Bishop Street, Honolulu, HI 96813 808-521-2731.

ILLINOIS
172 North Michigan Ave., Chicago, IL 60601 312-346-4228; 312-346-3240.

LOUISIANA
4403 Veterans Memorial Blvd., Metairie, LA 70006 504-887-7631;
   504-887-0113.

MASSACHUSETTS
50 St. Paul's Ave., Jamaica Plain, Boston, MA 02130 617-522-8911.
Rte. 1, 885 Providence Hwy., Dedham, MA 02026 617-326-5385.

MISSOURI
9804 Watson Rd., St. Louis, MO 63126 314-965-3512; 314-965-3571.

NEW JERSEY
561 U.S. Route 1, Wick Plaza, Edison, NJ 08817 908-572-1200.

NEW YORK
150 East 52nd Street, New York, NY 10022 212-754-1110.
78 Fort Place, Staten Island, NY 10301 718-447-5071; 718-447-5086.

OHIO
2105 Ontario Street (at Prospect Ave.), Cleveland, OH 44115 216-621-9427.

PENNSYLVANIA
214 W. DeKalb Pike, King of Prussia, PA 19406 215-337-1882; 215-337-2077.

SOUTH CAROLINA
243 King Street, Charleston, SC 29401 803-577-0175.

TEXAS
114 Main Plaza, San Antonio, TX 78205 210-224-8101.

VIRGINIA
1025 King Street, Alexandria, VA 22314 703-549-3806.

CANADA
3022 Dufferin Street, Toronto, Ontario, Canada M6B 3T5 416-781-9131.

AULD LANG SYNE

A Novella

JOHN A. VIKARA

The *Vandals series* titles:

The **V**andals

Adjuster

National **D**efense

Auld **L**ang **S**yne

Author's foreword

The characters and the events discussed in *Auld Lang Syne* were depicted in the previous trilogy.

I sat in front of the snowy screen of my television. The red-and-yellow station logo at the lower right corner of the screen, the only splash of color, stood vivid against an occasional gray shadow of movement through the streaks of windblown snow. From the time the announcer had described the unforeseen raging blizzard, I had become concerned for Gwen and her decision to drive home from New York. In our forty years of marriage, we had always spent New Year's Eve together, renewing our vows and planning for the coming year. I knew Gwen really wanted to be with me, but she had been compelled to make an emergency visit when her sister had unexpectedly taken ill two days earlier. She went alone, rather than burden me, with my chronic breathing problems, with the long, frigid trip. "Jimmy, you're staying home, and that's it!" she had said. I really couldn't psych myself up for the trip, so after a few minutes of manufactured dissent, I backed down and stayed home.

While she was in the area she had also visited

our son, Matt, a fireman and still a bachelor who lived
in Queens; then made a run to Long Island to see
Karen, our divorced daughter and her two children.
That was the last I had spoken with Gwen on the
phone, after also having welcomed conversations
with Paul and Timmy, our teenaged grandsons. It
probably hadn't started snowing when she left for
home, and she never listened to the car radio, so she
wouldn't have heard any warnings or forecasts. She
would be somewhere on the New York Thruway by
now, being buffeted by the heavy winds and blinding
whiteouts described on the newscast.

I had been alternately nodding off and jerking
my head upright for the last hour, desperately trying
to stay awake. I cleared my mind of the cobwebs and
dialed her cell phone number again. Static. Then
nothing. Then the static would again crackle through
the earpiece and change tone, until there was that
nothing again. No dial tone. No sound at all.
Everything outside the comfort and warmth of the
house had turned into a vast wasteland, this
description sometimes perceived about television
programming. And I was a prisoner of both
wastelands, the latter my only link to the happenings
in the outside world.

I hung up the receiver and decided I would
routinely try again every few minutes, hopeful that
the erratic dial tone would return, as it had—

2

momentarily—all through the day. Even better, that the phone would ring, and it would be Gwen with a status report, her account of being stranded somewhere but safe, her voice bringing relief for my jangled nerves. *Damn writer's imagination never lets go.* I needed to put those images of overturned cars in culverts out of my thoughts. My stomach churned. *Stop, already. She's smart enough and practical enough to know when to use good judgment. You have to quit imagining things like that. She's fine. I know it. I hope it.*

My sock-clad feet pattered softly over the living room carpet. The legs of my oversized blue sweatpants flapped against each other, and I nervously fiddled with the pull-string of my gray New York Mets sweatshirt. The blinds of the picture window that overlooked the front porch and driveway were open, but there was no scenery that wasn't covered in white. That stark crisp whiteness, moving like the shaken imitation snow inside one of those glass globes, shifted and swirled in unison with the smaller version on the television. Darkness had been premature and, together with the falling snow, now hid all the normal scenery.

That giant, bulky shadow could very well be some grotesque monster, a creature of the night with sinewy arms and icy fingers lurking there, ready to wrap those tentacles around people and hold them in the cold until they froze to death. I chuckled as I snapped on one of the three switches to the side of the doorjamb, and the two outside spotlights illuminated the gnarled branches and spindly twigs of our barren oak tree. Like I didn't know it was a tree! Just a little exercise in making the mind afraid of the dark. Hardly worth the effort. A more beneficial mental exercise would be to imagine the tree covered with green glossy leaves, shading the thirty-foot-long blacktop driveway that led to a sun-drenched street, surrounded by nothing but more green—green grass and green bushes with pastel-colored flowers and more green trees. Anything but white. I watched for a few minutes before being convinced that there were no headlights or snowplows out on the distant street.

I snapped off the spotlights and flipped the middle switch for the small exterior entry light beside the door. I was marooned for who knows how long—but my instincts considered this beacon cheaper to run than the spots. There were no Christmas lights or figurines for potential passers-by to notice. Not this year. What with Gwen's renewed arthritis and the outside frigid air grating at my ailing lungs, we had to abandon our usual decorating for the season. I may have felt the effects of loneliness less if I had some company, but our dog, a Doberman-Shepherd mix named Lady, had died at the beginning of December. I wished I had her love and

4

companionship with me now to tide me over until Gwen got home.

I turned and looked past the living room, through the open-floor setting of this side of the house—all in darkness—past the dining room, to the kitchen with the yellowish light in the vent above the stove and dots of red appliance lights and green LED numbers on the stove and microwave clocks. The back enclosed porch housed a small Christmas tree with twinkling minibulbs, a multicolored light at the end of a tunnel. I didn't need brightness to see. The light of the television and the flickering flame of the propane fireplace were enough to distinguish surroundings I had long since committed to memory. Besides that, I had remained practical into my old age, and the electric bill could stand a little trimming. I was perfectly satisfied with this atmosphere until Gwen returned home, bringing with her all the brightness needed.

As soon as her face flashed into my mind, the telephone receiver was in my hand. Nothing. Damn it. The stomach rolled again, more agitated with each passing minute. Was she okay? *Calm down. Sit. Relax.* I hung up and dropped onto the couch next to the telephone table. Maybe if I looked at another channel. All this whiteness was sleep-inducing, and I had to stay awake. It was like staring at a blank piece of paper and trying to write something that the brain couldn't materialize. I searched for the remote. I thought I had left it next to the phone. No. I felt between the cushions.

The flash of lightning was only a second before the crash of thunder that vibrated just outside the closest wall. The knickknacks on the fireplace mantle trembled, and the Christmas cards fluttered on their red string holder. Then the echo of the clap diminished, as into a long tunnel. *Damn!* I jerked my head toward the ceiling and saw the skylight—translucent by snow cover—brighten like a fog-shrouded crystal ball. The front window magnified and reflected the flash of the second bolt of lightning, overwhelming the illumination of the television screen. Another explosion of thunder followed, and I shuddered. *What the hell kind of storm is this? Thunder and lightning in a snowstorm?* I sat frozen for a minute, waiting for the next episode of the show. It never came. Twice was enough.

A harsh static snow had replaced the televised snow. The station logo was gone, along with the transmitted sound. *Damn! Now I'm really marooned!* I had seen the remote on the floor during the intensity of the lightning flashes. Yeah, there it was. I picked it up, sat back upright, and pushed the "channel select" button. The prickly dots disappeared, and there was Leo Gorcey smacking Huntz Hall with his hat. "What's the matter with you, you ignoramus," Muggs shouted at Glimpy, while the rest of the East Side Kids looked on. The black-and-white picture was sharp and clear. I was pleasantly surprised at the sight and smiled. *I think this is the one in the haunted house with Bela Lugosi.* I still remembered watching these movies on a nine- or ten-inch Dumont television when I was about eleven years old, squinting and straining my eyes. We were the last family on the block to get a TV, and that puny size was all my parents said they could afford. They were always so damn frugal that I had been sure—especially having seen some older scratches on the wooden cabinet—that it was either given to them or bought used.

I was less than happy with that time of my life. I had just moved back with them after strangers and an assortment of relatives had raised me during the war years—my father in the army, only seeing my mother on weekends. They were actually *the strangers* when we reunited. No effort was ever made by anyone to reclaim those lost years, and I could never feel any closeness to them. I tried desperately to *forgive and forget* through my life, but I was unable to completely shake those all-important formative years from my memory. My only escape was into movies like this. I felt a rush of apathy from my recollections. In spite of my enjoyment with the movie, I changed the channel.

Holy cow! *Hopalong Cassidy*. This was from my youth, too. *What's going on?* I couldn't believe the picture clarity, as I watched the silver-haired cowboy dressed in black and riding his white stallion, Topper, through the rugged landscape of the west. The picture was much clearer than when I had watched as a kid. *Well, of course. Better technology now.* What were the odds of two channels having movies from over sixty years ago? I pushed the button again, eerily anticipating another gem—and I wasn't disappointed. There was Soupy Sales with White Fang and Black Tooth. *What the hell is going on?* My mind reacted to the remote like it was some kind of voodoo doll, and it fell to the floor when I imagined it stunning my hand with an electric shock. The TV screen went blank.

"What's the matter, Jimmy, you don't like Soupy anymore? You used to love his show."

The voice was familiar, and…and it wasn't coming from the TV.

I twisted my upper torso as I jerked my head toward the rear of the house, feeling twinges of pain from both my sore neck and my intercostal rib muscles. I stared into the darkness, wondering how someone could have entered through the locked rear door. *Did I lock it?* I couldn't see any shapes other than the straight lines of the refrigerator and countertop. I would've felt a blast of cold air, even if the door had been opened only slightly.

"Somebody there?" I called.

No answer. *Maybe I'm going batty! Maybe I'm hearing things.* Well, I had better check the door to be sure.

I tried to turn off the imagination as I moved through the dining room, but for me it was like trying to blow out one of those trick birthday candles that relit with each breath. *No one's there. You were hearing things. These things happen when someone is isolated and feeling stress. Could someone be crouched down out of sight behind the counter?*

Nope! No one there. I slowed my pace as I cautiously stepped onto the back porch. It was colder than the other rooms, being the farthest from the fireplace. Could the voice have come from out there? A slight scent of pine from the dying tree still lingered in its corner, and the winking red and green tree lights reflected off the rear wall of windows, appearing to be an array of Christmas fireflies fluttering in the darkness outside. I looked around the small sparsely furnished room, verifying that, even in the dim light of the tree, there was no place to hide. I grasped the chilly lever of the metal and glass storm door and knew it was locked by the resistance to my downward push. I swiped my open hand across the wet glass and cupped my hands between the surface and my face. There wasn't an outer light at this door. *Great! What the hell—or who the hell—are you trying to see? It's dark out there.*

I turned away and headed to the fridge. *How about a beer? That should help.* I stopped in front of the white GE and, although I could barely see them in the amber stove light, squinted at the photos and magnetic plaques on its door. There were various scenes of the family from different phases of my life—Matt and Karen, Paul and Timmy, alone, in a group or posed with Gwen and me; a picture of my friend Jack from writing class; and an assortment of other friends. I had them memorized from the thousands of times I had stood here but still took comfort in seeing them, if only barely in the semidarkness.

Half of the kitchen lit up when I opened the door, and glass jars and bottles clinked against each other on the door shelves. There were five bottles of Bud on the top shelf, lined up between plastic bottles of 2 percent milk, diet soda, and spring water. *Well, beer is a health food, too. It's for my mental health.* I snatched one of the Buds.

I closed the door. My night vision was now seemingly more sensitive as I stared directly at a photo from my teens. As clear as daylight, there were

six of that *ol' gang o' mine*, the Vandals, including me
and my two best friends, Johnny and Pete Wilson. We
were about fifteen years old, all in dungarees and
wearing either black leather jackets or our black
woolen club jacket with a large aqua "V" on the right
breast. We were bunched into two groups, leaning
against the chain-link fence of our schoolyard
hangout. Johnny was resting his forearm on Pete's
shoulder, and I was standing between them and
Speedo, Sonny, and Crazy Lenny. I didn't remember
the picture, or having been there when it was taken,
and I suddenly wasn't even sure if I was actually
seeing the photo or if I was hallucinating from the
weird happenings of the last few minutes. I touched it
and found it to be real. Why was that photo there, and
who put it there, and when? If it was one of my many
keepsake photos, then it should be in my den with all
my other memorabilia.

I lifted a corner of the picture, and it seemed
to peel off the refrigerator door like a gummed
sticker. Beer in one hand, photo in the other, I
returned to the dining room and made a left into the
long hallway that led to the bedrooms, bathroom, and
the den. There were two nightlights plugged into
baseboard receptacles to light my way along the hall.

The hallway ended at the open doorway to the
den. I reached in and flipped the light switch. A soft-
white bulb in my desk lamp gave off a gentle glow,

and the walls, although shrouded by oblong shadows, came to life. Marlon Brando, *The Wild One*, sat atop a Triumph motorcycle. James Dean in his red jacket over white T-shirt, dungarees, and engineer boots leaned casually beside his sobriquet, *Rebel without a Cause*. Glen Ford and Sidney Poitier confronted Vic Morrow inside *The Blackboard Jungle*. They all graced the vertical surfaces of the room, along with other movie posters. Then there were my friends, less famous people than in the posters, but stars to me and much more important in my life, posed in framed photographs similar to the one in my hand. I took a swig of beer and placed the bottle on the desk. I searched the walls, as if I was looking for an open cage from where the picture might've escaped. They were all hanging where they should be. I slipped the photo into my sweatpants pocket.

"It wasn't from your collection," the mystery voice said, just as my peripheral vision sensed a movement in the hall.

I spun to face the doorway, a pang of fear slicing through my stomach. I reeled back into my desk at the sight of the image just outside the doorway. It was a male figure, but something about him was strange. I could…damn, I could see through him. My heart was pounding, and my breath sputtered in short, wheezing gasps. I tried to ask *what* and *who* and *how* and then looked more closely at the face. My

God! It was Speedo.

Speedo Moran. But he was killed in a car accident over fifty years ago. He was different from the photo I had just scrutinized. He was smiling, as in the photo, but he was older—maybe five years older—about the age he was when he died. He had the same curly black hair, contrasting his pale complexion with a small nose and ears on his round face atop a thin, five-foot-seven or -eight frame. My mind raced back to the night of that horrific crash, and yes, I remembered the clothes he had worn. It was the same black cloth Vandal jacket with the outline of clean material highlighting the missing "V" on the right breast.

"Don't ask me how, because I won't tell you, but I concocted the picture from memory and planted it on the refrigerator door," the Speedo image stated. His voice was human—no wavering or echo sound, like in low-budget ghost movies. "It got your attention like I wanted. You feel okay? You look kind of pale."

My mouth was open, but I couldn't form the words. I shook my head and thought I heard a rattle, like cartoon characters hear when trying to clear their thoughts; then I realized it was the air filtering from my suddenly phlegm-filled lungs. Why was this happening? Why all of a sudden would my past be haunting me? *Haunting? Great word choice.* I tried to move, first toward the figure, then to sit. My desk chair was within reach, but my muscles felt like they did an hour after shoveling snow. They stiffened and hardened, as if I was being frozen into an ice statue. My heart raced.

A singing group—the Quotations—was suddenly harmonizing their song, *Imagination,* and it streamed out of the speakers of my record/tape player on a table in another corner of the room. "Imagination is silly; it makes you go around willy-nilly—" Speedo flicked his wrist, and the music stopped. My muscles relaxed, and I slumped into my chair. My noisy breathing sounds were gone, and I was calm.

"That's what you think is happening," Speedo said. "You think you're imagining this. Well, you are in a way, 'cause if it wasn't for your imagination, you wouldn't be seeing me."

"So I am seeing you?" I finally questioned. "Or am I imagining I'm seeing you?"

"Both. You're seeing me in your mind. Kind of like that old question, if a tree fell in the forest and nobody was there to hear it, would it make a noise. If your mind wasn't fertile enough to see me, would you see me? You're seeing an image of me as you last remember me. I'm just an electrical impulse. Your mind has formed my image.

14

"You aren't looking too bad for an old guy. You kept your hair; and except for the gray on the temples and sideburns, it's still the same color as it was back when. Your face is fuller and a little wrinkled but hasn't changed so much that I didn't recognize you." His tone was cold, like he was giving a status report. "No stooped shoulders or hunched-over walk. Except for your emphysema, life has treated your body pretty well for the past seventy years."

"How'd you know I have emphysema?"

"I'll tell you later. But even with all of that praise, you still don't look too well. Is your breathing okay? How's your heart? Still pounding? Any pain?"

"No…" I felt my pulse. It was rapid but strong. "I think I'll survive."

"Good. We have a few things to talk about, and…"

I waited for him to finish his sentence. "And what?" I finally asked.

"Never mind. You'll see." He was still abrupt, out of character from what I remembered of his demeanor.

"Okay, well answer me this…why? Why is this happening?"

"The conditions have to be perfect. This freak storm, the unusual lightning, and our composition—like I said before, we're only like electrical impulses—everything has to click at once for something like this to happen. The movies aren't too far off when they show ghosts appearing on a stormy night."

"No, man. I mean, why do you want to be here? Why do you want to talk to me?"

"It's New Year's Eve. No one should be alone on New Year's Eve." Again, his tone was not his; he was merely uttering a flat unemotional statement.

"Well, thanks, but Gwen is on her way. I won't be alone for long."

"It'll be awhile before she gets here."

"What?"

"Because of the storm. It's not going to stop soon."

"Oh, alright. Don't scare me like that," I said, relaxing my tensed shoulder muscles. "And there's gotta be more to this than you coming to keep me company for New Year's Eve."

"Well, we can see you still have a lot of issues from the past that you keep bottled up inside, like a

16

lot of things that you never reacted to in the past because you didn't—"

"Didn't have the guts?!" A flash of red clouded my eyes, as a rush of old memories leaped from my unconsciousness. "You're here to chastise me because some people thought I didn't have the guts I needed to be one of the Vandals?"

"Hey, there's guts for being aggressive, and there's guts that show a different kind of toughness, a toughness of mind that gets people through life without having to prove themselves every time someone looks at them funny. But…" he paused, and although his features were hidden in the darkness, not sharp enough for me to see an expression, I could sense he was contemplating something that required a thoughtful decision.

"Do you remember the time you were part of the group that took on those crazy revolutionaries at their stronghold?" Speedo asked abruptly.

Oh, oh. Something's wrong here. "God, how could I forget?"

"Well, I'm here to…to get you to tell me why you ran out on the guys when the shooting started."

His bluntness overwhelmed me. My breath caught in my throat for an instant. *Why would*

17

someone want to bring that incident up after all these years? I couldn't admit that I was a lousy coward; that I had lost my nerve—if only for the moment—because it was the first time I had ever faced gunfire. The roar of the gunshots ringing in my ears, the smell of the cordite, the bodies falling, the blood…it was too much. My mind had gone numb, and I was carried away from the nightmarish scene by the will to survive.

I proved myself after that; I helped the mission to be successful; it was a split-second loss of composure. No way will I admit…Wait a minute. I never told anyone; I never confided in anyone about what I did. Everyone just thought I had got lost in the heat of battle.

"Ran? Who said I ran?"

"You know you did! They know you did. All they want you to do is admit it."

"They? Who are they? I don't know what you're talking about."

"I can't tell you who…" His voice began to crack, to mellow. "Jimmy, please, gimme a break. I don't want to do this. They sold me a bill of goods. They…"

The window on the other side of the room lit

up, and a roll of thunder echoed and vibrated through the pane.

"Jimmy, they're mad at me. Don't make me tell you. I only have a short time here to do what they want me to, but I...I just can't make myself go through with it. You were my friend." He was Speedo again; the one I remembered as my friend. "I'm kind of stuck in the middle now."

"What can I do?"

"Forget about all those things from your past, all those things that you keep dredging up that drive you crazy. Stop blaming your family life and believing that they made you an introvert with low self-esteem and unable to cope. If you get rid of those burdens, then you can also put that...that incident that you say didn't happen out of your thoughts. Get rid of the pent-up hate and find the peace you need to resist them. Then they won't have an avenue into your mind to exploit it."

"That's not very easy for me."

Speedo had hit a nerve when he said that I had bottled-up issues bugging me, a lot of hostility and somewhat of a bruised ego, and he certainly knew it, too—from my outburst. My frustrations were triggered by recalling events where I thought I should've reacted in a certain way, feelings that should've been resolved years ago. Mostly that one incident in particular, the incident that he said he was here to bring into the open. I had always heard that a person's memory faded with old age. Mine was too fertile, and many times it reenacted those past events, trying to change the outcome or justify my actions to put my mind at ease, questioning my deeds to the point of self-loathing. The only person who could ever put my mind at ease was Gwen. And I never told her about that time. I was that ashamed of it. Gwen...

"I have to try to reach Gwen, Speedo. You gotta let me—"

"She's fine for now," Speedo said.

"For now? What's going on?"

"She's fine, period. There's nothing wrong, and you can try her again soon," Speedo said. "Please give me what time I have left here to help you. It's probably the only way I have to redeem myself."

"With who?"

"Where I am—where we all are—is limbo. To get out of limbo, we have to earn points. We have to complete deeds to earn points. It isn't like being locked up. There's plenty of freedom there. Maybe too much. It's like doing penance, just hanging around looking for something to do, kind of like when we hung out on the street corner waiting to grow up. I really miss tinkering with cars and all the little things that keep a person's mind occupied. As you may have noticed, I have a lot better vocabulary than the last time you saw me. I try to pick up some little tidbit of knowledge from anyone that passes through. I know I can earn some brownie points by counseling you, my good deed to go into my bank. Sometime in the future, when I accumulate enough credits, I may be allowed to pass through the tunnel—"

"Tunnel? What tunnel?"

"The one we all hope to pass through someday, toward the light at the end. Look, I can't tell you everything, or I'll really screw myself—with everyone. What got me into this bind with you is my need to get a fatter bank balance. Call it greed or an obsession to get the hell out of my situation, but I was offered ten times more credits by appearing to you than I can by what I'm doing now, trying to helping you out. But like I said, down inside…I'm not someone who screws his friends."

"And I appreciate that. I knew there was something wrong, something that wasn't you. I guess once you're given a personality, it stays with you forever. So who the hell approached you and why do they want me to…to, you know?"

"Jimmy, I'm sorry, but I still gotta go back and

21

live with these guys. Don't push me on it. My only part in it was to get you to verbally admit that deed. I don't know their reason, but I know it's something that's not good for you. I was long dead when that incident happened, so I don't know what they're talking about. Let's just take what time I have left to instead talk about the good things from our past."

"To tell you the truth," I said to Speedo, becoming more comfortable with his presence and trying to push out the gathering black clouds in my mind, "I had no life until I met you guys. You all taught me how to have fun. The kids on my block treated me like a *schmuck* after my parents finally took me back and we moved into our new neighborhood. I was never good at any sports. No one in my family taught me shit, except maybe how to pinch pennies and complain about how bad things were. *That* they were good for. At that time of my life, I was the most naïve person around. It took years to educate me out of that routine. I spent three years trying to be good at stickball and basketball and even shooting bottle caps, but I could never lose that image of being the low man on the totem pole, the little jerk that couldn't do anything worthwhile."

"The asshole jocks that treated you like that would never have made it with us," Speedo said. "So we rescued you, hah?"

"You sure did. My whole life changed when I hooked up with the Vandals. Maybe I couldn't immediately shake the inferiority complex I had developed, but I became respected for being me, not something superficial like how I could throw a ball. I also found a new meaning for family, a lot different than the apathy at home."

"Yeah, we did have our own little family on the street," Speedo said. "The saying is, friends are the family you choose—but no matter how close some of us were, you still couldn't replace your real family. I mean, they provided you with a home, and that's what it's all about. You have to let go of those misconceptions and confusion about your family that you're still carrying around."

"Like another saying says, a house is not a home. It takes more than shelter and food to survive what's in store for a person in life. I was a latchkey kid, trying to fend for myself most of the time. They were seldom around, because they were too busy working longer hours for crap wages and never tried to better their existence. They were happy as long as there was enough left over for their idea of recreation—sitting in some bar on weekends.

"They'd drag me along, buy me a Coke, and pack me away in an out-of-the-way table in a corner, like I was some piece of luggage being stored away for the night. The clouds of cigar smoke in the place could choke a horse. I often wondered why the hell I started smoking after having my young lungs exposed to that environment. I would be sitting there, minding my own business, drawing my little comic books, making up stories as an escape, when their drunken friends would come parading by me on the way to the toilet and blow their booze breath in my face. The women would call me *cutie* and pinch my cheek, and the men would make some kind of joke about me or ponder why I wasn't out playing ball. When I didn't answer their stupid, incoherent questions, they'd mutter that I must have something wrong with me or they'd tell my mother that I was impolite. She would frown, tell them *You know how kids are these days,* and then later jump on my ass because I embarrassed them in front of their friends. I mean, one minute they're telling you to be seen and not heard, and the next they're on your case for doing exactly what they told you to do.

"Every time someone at the bar laughed and glanced over at me, well, I...I was sure they were talking about me. I felt like that guy in a carnival with his head sticking out of a hole in a canvas and getting balls thrown at him. The center of attention for a bunch of drunks who had someone weaker than them to pick on. Not much different from how it was out in the world of the neighborhood jocks. They each needed someone to feel superior to, so they wouldn't be considered on the bottom of the pecking order.

"That and other shots at my ego were the foundation of my life. So tell me why I developed into an unsettled introvert. You know those are the developmental backgrounds of some serial killers. They should be glad I didn't turn into a serial killer. I guess that would have *really* embarrassed them.

"All I wanted was for them to show some love. I know we weren't in the habit of saying anything like that back then. It wasn't the accepted thing to discuss between a father and son and sometimes not even with a mother. The fact is that we weren't like *Ozzie and Harriet* and *Father Knows Best* and all those bullshit TV shows back then. We were living the real life."

"Hey, we're supposed to be talking about the good things from our past. Everyone always remembers the bad stuff and very seldom sees the little enrichments hidden in the fog that shape both people and events behind the scenes," Speedo said. "Weren't you scared to go home if you got into some petty trouble? Didn't you hate someone to say *I'm gonna tell your mother on you?* Didn't you wish you had acted differently when you got into bigger trouble with us and had problems with the law? That's because deep down, you still respected them and didn't want to let them down."

I unconsciously nodded in agreement, but then said, "Sure, because they were quick to blame. You know how it was back then. If an adult said you did something wrong, then you were guilty. They didn't want any trouble. They didn't want their little lifestyle interrupted by some outside influence."

"Like no one else had it as bad as—or worse than—you? Well, you know who did? They did! And everyone before them. So from their experiences, they felt that they were doing the best things for you. And whether it only sometimes showed, or never showed, they were still doing it from their hearts. You were a latchkey kid, because they were busy putting food on the table and keeping a roof over your head, and you were with them on weekends, so—no matter how it looked on the surface—you wouldn't be home alone, and they could appreciate your company. That was their way of showing their love."

He was right. Not that this was some kind of epiphany. I'm sure I always knew it, but I still used it to feel sorry for myself or put the blame for my shortcomings on others. But the thing that really bothered me was that I never developed the balls to get it done every time, all the time, not in just the everyday grind needed to get through life. I still had that passive DNA, that need to avoid any conflicts that I could squirm out of, and that's why I ran…*No! Don't think about that time. He said to forget it. Put it out of your mind.*

"Hey, man, thanks for getting me to maybe look at things a little different. But what made you such an advocate of parents?" I asked, trying to shift the onus of the conversation, trying to stuff those flawed decisions back into the recesses of my mind. "You were always getting into fights with your father and coming around with a fat lip or black eye. You literally lived on the street for most of your teens because you didn't want to go home."

"We had our reconciliation," Speedo said. "We met when they got here, and I found that their past was—like I said before—what guided their way of life and all the lives of most generations. You have a lot of time where I am now to make things right."

"Look, man, I'm really into all this, but—"

"But you gotta try to reach Gwen."

"What are you, reading my mind?"

"You've been fidgeting in your chair and constantly looking towards the other room where your phone is. Not much guessing why. Gimme just a few more minutes. I don't have much time left here."

I sighed and tried to move my legs. I was still

pinned to the seat. "Okay…but I'm really concerned about her…"

"The fifty years I've been there is a blink of an eye as it relates to eternity. All I'm asking for is a couple more minutes, like a millisecond of eternity. As I said before, I'm hoping that my time will be reduced by helping you to understand what really happened in your life."

"And I hope it helps you, too, but…Well, okay. Speaking of fifty years ago, I couldn't believe how you and Shades Gaglione bought it, running from the cops for something you didn't do. You were the best wheelman in the crowd. How—"

"Too fast, not enough time to stop when I saw traffic in front of me as I rounded that bend."

"What became of Shades Gaglione? Is he around there with you?"

"Shades prefers to stay in a different area. I've only seen him a couple of times since we've been there, and that's because he still won't forget what I did. He's still pissed at me for getting him killed—as you might expect—and he's having a hard time getting over it. Like, what's the worst he could do, *kill me*?" He paused, probably wondering about his attempt at humor. "It's going to take a lot longer for him to move on. He isn't an evil entity, but you know

28

he could be a vicious guy back then. All entities have a trace of evilness, just enough to give us aggressiveness and the instinct for survival. Shades had a tad more than usual, and a person like that either does a lot of time or, under certain rules and circumstances, gets rescheduled for another in-body round on earth."

Speedo had never been much of a talker until you got him started on a subject that he was familiar with. "Rescheduled?" I pressed.

"Well, there's only a few trillion or so personalities in existence. Like, how many miniscule nuances can there be before producing two entities exactly the same. The trillions were originally used up a long time ago and had to be constantly recycled. After a century or so, every entity that passes through here has either served a long—and in my opinion, borrrrring—sentence and passes through the tunnel to the final reward or, if approved by the rules committee, is put back into a body to try again. A second chance. What some people call reincarnation. We call it in-body when you're…well, in a body.

"The pure evil entities are controlled by Satan and his demons in Hell, which has several other planes of existence. They have a converse trace of good that tempers their personalities and keeps them from destroying everyone and everything they come in contact with. Every once in a while one of their kind escapes to in-body with an unadulterated evil persona, like Hitler or Stalin. The demons have the power to automatically reincarnate their hordes, because there's less of them. They also have the power to go on and on, constantly screwing up the world."

The window on the other side of the room again rattled from a clap of thunder.

"Man, please don't ask anymore. Now you're getting me in trouble with the rules committee, the guys who have the power to approve my credits."

"I'm sorry." I held my hands in front of me and looked around the room, hoping there was some signal I could give to show it was my fault for Speedo's indiscretion.

"There's just time enough for me to enlighten you about one more thing."

A dog barked at the other end of the hall.

"Lady?" I asked, wanting to stand and go to her. My legs wouldn't move.

"No," Speedo said. "She hasn't processed through yet. It takes about a month or so by your time. That's Rexy, your first pet."

"Rexy?" My eyes began to fill. "That poor guy. Why did you have to bring him into this? I was just beginning to warm up to my parents, and you screw up my head with Rexy? They always kept him chained up outside, no matter what the weather, in a cold doghouse. How was he a pet with those restrictions? The worst thing was when they were getting complaints from the landlord about his barking. As usual, they didn't want any trouble with anybody, so it was more convenient to call the pound and have him taken away. They didn't give a crap about my feelings—about how I felt when I saw him being dragged away, how he looked back at me with those sad eyes, wondering why this was happening to him, what he had done to me to deserve this. Some son of a bitch in my neighborhood told me later that they probably gassed him because he was only a mutt. What the hell did he ever do to them?"

"Look closer," Speedo said. "Look down the hall."

I strained my eyes against the dimness of the far end of the hall and could see two dark shapes. No, three. One was small. Rexy?

"That's your parents," Speedo said. "I met them when they befriended my folks. They wanted me to see you and kind of be their spokesman. It's one of the reasons I couldn't go through with what I

31

originally came here for. I promised them I'd talk with you.

"They have Rexy with them. Your father got here first but waited until your mother joined him before they went looking for Rexy in the animal-plane, to bring him back here and be with them. They wanted to redeem themselves for what they did to him while in-body. He's very happy with them, and they love and care for him."

"Oh, man." I bowed my head and my eyes filled again. "I'm sorry." I raised my head. "Why don't they come in here? Don't they want to talk to me?"

"They aren't in a state of mind to talk with you yet. It will take a little longer for them to realize that you no longer have that animosity for them."

I suddenly felt the love for them that I should've been feeling my entire life, not a gushing love, as I was sure that expressiveness wasn't in our genes, but a love of feeling closer and more connected. I tried to work up a smile. I didn't know how it showed on my face but hoped it looked as sincere as possible. I slowly raised my hand and waved. "Thanks," I said. "Thanks for everything."

The murky images faded, blended into the overall darkness, and were gone.

"I wish I could've seen them, spoken to them, apologized…"

"They understand," Speedo said. "Everything will be okay. One more thing I wanted you to know—remember how you used to chain smoke, could never quit no matter how hard you tried?"

I nodded, feeling tightness in my chest. "One of my stupid acts of rebellion, which became a habit and came back to bite me in the ass when I got older."

"Well, when entities first pass out of their bodies, they have twenty-four hours before they're released from the earth's surface; and during that time, or upon arriving there, they kind of get a choice. They can make something happen on earth but have to accept a longer stay here in limbo. Not something dramatic like world peace. Some little personal gesture. Your mom's choice was to have you quit smoking."

"Yes. Yes, that's right; I did finally stop about a month after she died."

"Her choice helped you to quit. That's how I knew you had emphysema," Speedo said. "Her sacrifice has cost her, and your father who chose to stay with her, more time there before they can move onto the tunnel. She saved your life. You would've been there with us a dozen years ago instead of sitting here, albeit afflicted with emphysema."

I took a shallow breath and shook my head. "I...don't know...what to say. All of this revelation is just so overwhelming. Believe me, if you are truly doing this to change my attitude, you're succeeding."

"Good. You're stronger now; more capable of facing the danger that's ahead. I'm only part of what's happening tonight. There's definitely going to be a follow-up."

I stared at Speedo. He seemed more transparent than a minute ago. "You mean I'm going to be visited by ghosts from the present and future?" I asked, trying to breeze over Speedo's ominous comments.

"No, Mr. Scrooge," Speedo said picking up on my inference. "Only from your troubled past. No one here knows the future. Only you can shape that."

"Who's coming next? Anyone I know?"

"Yep. He'll be here soon. Y'know, this little talk we just had...well, you were always a good guy. I feel kind of...kind of funny about what I was trying to do to you. I'm sorry, Jimmy. Just be careful of what you say in the next couple of hours. Okay?"

Speedo's image was the clarity of rippling water. He flicked his wrist, and his hand seemed to turn into the limpid flow of a waterfall, as the speakers on the opposite side of the room sprang to life with the voices of the Cadillacs. *"Well now, they often call me Speedo, but my real name is..."* He was gone before I could ask him about his closing remarks.

I found I could suddenly move. I took a swallow of beer and then raised the bottle in a salute. "I hope you get to that tunnel real soon. If you can, bring my family with you. If it's possible for me to get an IOU on my future credits, use it for them, and that will be my gift back to Mom for keeping me alive. I'll catch up eventually."

I pressed harder on the bottle and felt the intense cold of the glass. It was real; I took another drink to prove it, then put the bottle on my desk. I pinched my leg. *Ouch!* Wasn't that the old tried-and-true method to see if you were dreaming? *No, I'm not asleep on the couch in front of the television. It did happen. It...* The telephone rang in the kitchen, further proving the reality of my surroundings. It rang again as I slipped, trying to get out of the chair. I twisted my ankle as I stood. I hopped on one foot—*fomp, fomp, fomp* down the carpeted hall. *I should've put an extension in the den.*

It must have rung five or six times before I reached it. Leaning against the counter, panting and

35

wheezing from the exertion, I snatched the receiver from the cradle. *Damn!* It had gone into message mode. The stupid system didn't allow for speaking to the caller once it went to the message phase. *We should've upgraded the system.*

"Gwen!" I gasped for breath. "Is…is that you?" Even if it was her, I knew she couldn't hear me, and I was only shouting from frustration. I would have to wait until the message ended and the red indicator light came on. I pushed the bad air from my leathery lungs in three long exhales before I could breathe easier. *There's the light!* I poked the replay button.

"Jimmy, where are you?" It *was* Gwen. "Jimmy? I'm stuck at a…stop. I can't…home. I'll try you again. Please pick up…phone when…call. I love…" The damn static wiped out the remainder of the message. Then the lousy nothing. I kept pressing and releasing the cradle lever, but it was hopeless. The damn thing was down again. At least I knew she was safe somewhere. I waited for a couple minutes before picking up the receiver again and found the dead silence was still screaming in my ear. I hung up and limped into the living room.

I sat on the couch where I had been before, next to the extension phone. I checked the phone line again. Still nothing. I took the Combivent inhaler from my sweatpants pocket and took a couple of puffs, picked up the television remote, and pushed the power button. The screen flashed bright before settling to its normal hue, but without a picture. *What oldie but goodie show was going to pop on?* I pressed the channel select button.

Oh, wow! It was Zacherle, the Cool Ghoul. His thin face was made-up with dark smudges under his eyes and on his cheeks, which,   although obviously fake, made his face appear even gaunter. His dark hair was parted in the middle, and he wore an undertaker's frock coat. He and his entourage were seated on the set of a crypt. He gave that forced laugh of his and then said, "And now, back to *Mighty Joe Young.*"

The segment of the movie showed cowboys trying to lasso and subdue the giant gorilla. Joe was holding his own, and he would slam down any of the cowboys who got too close to him. Just as one of the cowboys flew out of the frame, the scene shifted to a set with skimpy props, obviously not even close to replicating the jungle locale of the movie. A figure tumbled onto the set and leaped to his feet. It was Zacherle. He raised his fist, shook it, and shouted, "You big ape!" The movie immediately resumed, leaving me in stitches.

He was a pisser. He was famous for his break-

37

ins; injecting himself into whatever movie he was showing. *Thank you, Speedo—or whoever was sending me these cherished good memories.* As soon as I started getting my head into the movie, it was gone, replaced by another of my favorite comedians, Ernie Kovacs, who was doing one of his characters, *Percy Dovetonsils.* Man, if anything could relieve the stress of this day, it was all these great black-and-white clips coming over that television set.

Suddenly, it was back to *Mighty Joe Young.* Just as suddenly back to the studio set. But it wasn't Zacherle standing under the fake palm tree this time. It was…yeah, it was Sonny Kraus, another of my Vandal buddies. He was about thirty years old, much older than he would've been in relation to this Zacherle show. He was wearing his trademark skin-tight black T-shirt that showed off his bulging arms.

"Surprise!" Sonny shouted. He turned sideways and flexed his muscles, and then the movie was back on the screen.

"Let's see Speedo do that," Sonny said from the couch that was aligned perpendicular to mine.

I flinched, startled at the unexpected appearance of someone sitting ten feet away. *So this is my next visitor. Is he going to be as blunt as Speedo tried to be? Is he gonna pop the question right off? What's his game? Whatever, I'll play along for now.*

Sonny had that ever-present confident smile as he stared at me, perhaps waiting for a verbal retort to his boast. At thirty years old, he still had had a modified pompadour hairstyle with the sides slicked back. Dark circles under his eyes and just a trace of pockmarks on his cheeks accented his ruggedly handsome features, resembling a mixture of a young Vic Morrow and Richard Burton. He had continued his teenage obsession of bodybuilding during the ten years he spent in prison, until the day he died at that godforsaken radical militia fortress back in 1969, the place I had to put out of my mind.

"Yeah, Jimmy, it's me," Sonny said. "I'm here to fill you in on the real picture. Speedo's a nice guy, but you know and I know that he was a little naïve and just a little too sensitive. I mean, the only thing he was good at was souping up cars and racing—and look what that did for him."

"Well, hell, I was kind of like him, too," I offered.

"Maybe when you first showed up looking to be a Vandal, but we changed your outlook on things."

"Yeah, that's for sure…but not what was buried deep inside."

"You had it right when you talked with Speedo before. It was your bringin' up before you met us that screwed up your head. You were sheltered from life. You never had any confidence in yourself."

"Let's not go back there," I said. "Speedo helped me to make peace with my family."

"So there is something else bothering you other than the screwed-up head you came to us with?"

"Sure, there's torments that people carry with them…" *Remember, nothing about that incident.* "…things that they don't want to discuss with anyone else."

"Hey," Sonny said in a soothing voice, "Let it out. I'm not a body sitting here. I'm in your head. You're talking to only you. So…there's things you wouldn't tell a priest in a confessional, or a psychiatrist—or your mate? You don't tell her everything?"

"No." *He's trying. Yeah, he was there when it happened. Is he the one who's orchestrating this little witch-hunt? What was it Speedo kept rushing things for? He didn't have much time here. I'm sure that applies to Sonny's visit, too. If I can keep him talking about other things, maybe he'll eat up his time before…* "Not stuff that I'm not proud of, stuff that doesn't affect our life together. I don't want her helping me to carry my past burdens."

"That's the stuff you're supposed to share. Maybe Speedo did make some inroads with you. You know you should forget—or better yet, be forgiven and forget."

"Forgiven? I don't need to be forgiven for anything."

"There may be things you don't realize you should be forgiven for."

"There are things about me that only I need to know. Maybe they're unwarranted and maybe not. Speedo did help me to see something about my existence. I've done things that I'm not proud of, but I've also done good things or made efforts that I was never rewarded for, so I figure by this time in my life they're all balanced out."

I don't know if he believes that. I know I don't. I must have strained my conscience.

"Maybe you weren't Johnny-on-the-spot when something went down, but when you knew you had to be stand-up because it meant something, then you were there. Like when you had to fight me as part of your initiation. You know, you were one of only two guys to give me a bloody nose. The other guy was Kelly, the president of the Vandals—who *I* had to fight to get in the club. Exclusive company you were in."

41

"Lucky punch. You know it, and everyone else knew it. Besides that, I saw the wink you and Johnny exchanged after it was over. I knew you took it easy on me, because he was sponsoring me and asked you for a favor."

Sonny's smile broadened. "That's not the point here. You were a skinny hundred-and-forty-pound skeleton, but you didn't think twice about the challenge, even though you knew you might get pounded into the ground." His bicep twitched to—intentionally or not—emphasize his 'David and Goliath' example. "You wanted something. You wanted to be a Vandal, and you were willing to take a beating to get it."

I thought about that day, about Sonny standing over me as I lay in the dust and dirt of a vacant lot, bruised face and bruised ego. I thought I'd be laughed at, but I was lifted to my feet, congratulated—*for getting my ass kicked*—and declared to be a Vandal. My ego had soared, and I'd never forget that day.

"Whatever it was that was bothering you inside your head back then made you kind of unique. It made you cool, like James Dean. I know he was your favorite back then, and guess what…I saw him, where we are. You wouldn't want to be like him anymore. He's still a rebel—but also still lost. He can't get his head on straight and wanders aimlessly, as if he's in a daze. Now, you don't want that for yourself, so you better get things worked out inside that noggin of yours before it's too late."

A chill ran up my spine, as if something unpleasant was coming. "Meaning what?"

Sonny held his hand out like a traffic cop. The flickering light of the fireplace danced around his fingers as if they were bulbs in a fiery crystal chandelier. "I just wanted to tell you about James Dean." He dropped his hand, but the iridescent flickering lingered in front of his face for another moment. "I also want to help you get rid of all the crap you have pent up in your mind. That's why I'm here."

"Oh? Just why are you guys *really* here? Speedo said you wanted me to admit something? He tap-danced all around it, and now you're saying you wanted to tell me about James Dean. So you drop in, using a once-in-a-blue-moon phenomenon to get here, wasting this unique opportunity to let me dig up my past—and to tell me about *James Dean?*"

Oh, damn. Now you went and done it. Well, let's get it out in the open and be done with it, already.

"Okay. You were always a sharp guy." Sonny held up his hand again, and the shimmer of the flames

43

seemed to dance off his fingertips and settle into his eyes, making them glow like red-hot coals for an instant. "We need to get some brownie points. Speedo told you that, right?"

I nodded.

"The points are for our redemption. You know that the reason I talked my way into that gig that got me killed was to redeem myself for the way I screwed up back when we were kids, to make up for getting the Vandals busted and the club broken up."

"But you did redeem yourself. You helped make the mission a success. You almost made it out. If it wasn't for that crazy girl who shot you…"

Sonny laughed sardonically. "Yeah. You being a writer, you must've seen the irony in my death. Shot by a broad who was the kid sister of the bitch that…well, I'll admit it, the bitch who seduced me into falling for her little revenge scheme and causing the downfall of the Vandals. If I had never hooked up with the bitch in the first place, I wouldn't have been trying to be redeemed, and I wouldn't have been killed by her sister a dozen years later."

"Yeah, I get it. But what's all this got to do with brownie points now, and what's it got to do with me?"

Sonny's hand was up again, pointing at me, the orange and blue flicker running the length of his arm. "Like I said before, you never pushed yourself into anything unless you really wanted something badly. Then you'd fight for it. And that's exactly what you did that time, when you dogged us and put your ass in the line of fire so you could be there to help your friends, even when everyone told you to get lost—and you weren't doing it to make a buck, like most of us were there for. You were doing it 'cause you just had to back up your best buddies, Johnny and Pete." For an instant, I saw Sonny's eyes as two red-hot coals again from the fireplace reflection.

"Sure, I was an adult by then, so I had ratcheted up my courage a little." *Easy. Measure your words.* "I'd never sat out when I thought I could help…and I guess I had to prove something to myself once more. Kind of like a preview of a midlife crisis."

"And you did! When you needed to be counted on, you were there."

"Yeah? So…so then why the hell am I being…*interviewed* by you guys?"

"Interviewed. Hah, that's rich."

"Damn it, let's get this over with. You want me to admit I ran out on the fight? Well, I won't. I didn't do anything wrong, and I'm not admitting to doing anything wrong. And besides, you were killed later—by that girl. Why would what I did have anything to do with you?"

"You mean later than the fight inside the headquarters building?"

"Yeah. Why would you care if I ran or didn't run? You got out of there. It was Crazy Lenny who died because he couldn't get away. Why—"

"He died because he *couldn't get away*, because there was one less gun there to—"

"One less gun? I never fired a shot. I wasn't even armed. How could you count on me? It was the first time I was ever in the middle of a gunfight. How could you count on me?"

"So you were scared? Unlike Lenny, you could get away. You had to get the hell out, right?"

The memories poured back into my mind; the felling of panic, of helplessness, of overwhelming fear. I had to get rid of those agonizing pictures in my mind. Admit it already. What can they do to you?

"So you did run?"

"I panicked." I felt the years of carrying that load melt, seemingly turn into vapor and float from my body. "Everyone thought I just got lost in the shuffle when we all separated."

"You never told this to anyone before, because you know you did something wrong?" Sonny's voice had hardened to that of an interrogator.

"No. I mean, yes, I did something wrong, but you have to consider—"

"You were ashamed of what you did?"

"Yeah. After it happened, I…I wandered around inside that massive abandoned factory for a while…I finally realized I was there for a purpose. Those crazy bastards we were fighting were going to kill hundreds of people with that poison gas, and my future wife, Gwen, was going to be one of those victims. I had to pull myself together and get back into the fight. I had to stop them from killing her, from killing anyone. *We* had to stop them—"

"See, I told you I had you pegged. I said you only get your back up when it means something." He glanced quickly over my shoulder. "Except for Lenny getting killed, you didn't really do anything wrong," Sonny said, with a hint of sarcasm. "I mean, after all, you did come back—"

"But, in the meantime, I was dead," a new voice growled from behind me.

There were no footfalls or even a whisk of

shadow rushing by me, but in an instant he was there, sitting next to Sonny. It was Crazy Lenny.

"So you finally admit you ran out on us," Lenny said, with an overtone of satisfaction in his raspy voice. "I saw you disappear down that rear hallway while we still needed every man to pull his weight."

I was stunned into silence, being more shocked at seeing Lenny than I had been with the previous two spirits. Lenny was a scary guy. He was about the same height as Sonny, nowhere as muscular, but his dark, slicked-back shiny hair and long, pointy face, which came to an apex at the tip of his nose, gave him a menacing air. His thin lips, constantly in a frown, gave the appearance of a shark; and I almost expected that if he did part his lips to any noticeable degree, shards of jagged teeth, in place of his own, would flash into view. He wore the same brown cracked leather jacket, black shirt, and black denim trousers as when I had last seen him.

"Cat got your tongue?" Lenny asked.

No, a shark. "I—I didn't expect…"

"Yeah, I guess you didn't. Well, I'm here, and you're gonna pay for what you did to me."

"Pay? What do you mean? It wasn't like I was

the one who shot you. In fact, I went back for your body when things calmed down."

"Small consolation." Lenny pursed his lips into a thin, wrinkled circle. "That was the very least you could do, after I agreed to let you stick around—even though I knew deep down that you would punk out. I never liked you from when we were kids. I never liked you hiding behind Johnny. You just didn't seem to be one of us. You were too damn sensitive. You came back for my carcass to ease your conscience for what you did, not for anything else."

"I don't know...maybe." I looked away. "Yes, I did run. Yes, damn it! All these years I couldn't forget that night. But I can't believe that it was the cause of you getting killed." I turned back. "You were staying behind because of your injured foot. You couldn't get out without...without help."

"Oh, really?" Lenny looked smug, probably enjoying his torment of me. "So if you had stayed and helped me, you think the outcome may have been different?"

"There were others who could've helped you. They told me later that you chose to stay behind, to give covering fire so they could get away. You were a hero."

49

Lenny scoffed at the compliment. "What nobody else knew was that while the shooting was going on around me—while I was concentrating on you instead of paying attention to the fight, watching you slither away and cursing your damn hide—I caught a bullet in the liver. I knew I was a dead man, so I stayed to cover the other guys while they got away."

"What about the guy who actually shot you? Why can't you go after him?"

"He's long gone. In fact, I met him where we are, and guess what—he was killed by one of your bullets later that day. Isn't that a blast?"

"Well, there you go. I took out the guy that killed you. Doesn't that settle the score?"

"Sorry. It doesn't work that way. First, it was a coincidence, not your deed of revenge. Second, I'm entitled to take the place of someone who got me killed, and *you* are the only living contributor.

"I could've blown you away when we were alone before the firefight," Lenny went on. "Maybe I should've. No witnesses. I could've told everybody that the clowns we were fighting knocked you off. The only reason I let you live was so you could help me across to that meeting. I couldn't walk, but I had to be there, and you were the only one around. You got me there; it was your job to help get me back. I spared your life, and that's how you repaid me?"

That revelation floored me. All these years I had thought that we had parted...not friends, certainly, but with an arms-length agreement. I had tried to remember him as a budding friend, and all the while...

"I'm sorry...I'm really sorry you died feeling that way. But—"

"No buts, man. You helped get me killed by your actions and I'm calling in your marker. I'm entitled to go back in-body at your expense."

"What?"

"Oh, yeah, Speedo didn't know about *that.* If he did, his big mouth would've spilled it. He was ready to get yanked outta there for just what he did say.

"And I'm telling you right now!" Lenny shouted to the ceiling, "You ain't getting my points like I promised you. You hear that, you little shit? You blew it!"

"I don't understand."

"If someone causes or contributes to another entity's death, the entity that passed on can—under

certain circumstances—have the offender or a
suitable replacement take his place. That's how it's
written, word for word, in the governing laws."

"What governing laws? What about God? I
would think He would be the only governing being,
and I don't think He would approve of anything like
that."

"We don't talk about Him. His domain is on
the other side of the tunnel, where the light comes
from. Neither He nor Satan has any influence on our
plane. A separate set of rules were negotiated eons
ago, and a rules committee was put in place to
enforce them. Everyone there will serve their time
under those rules until they pass through the tunnel,
go back in-body, or do something really horrendous, I
mean something so bad that they'd be sent down to
Hell."

"Well, what you're trying to do is horrendous.
I don't feel that I contributed to your death, and I
won't cooperate with your rules. Do you have the
power to make me die? Are you going to kill me?
You mean to tell me that sometime back in ancient
history God negotiated and then approved of killing a
living being in order to take their place? I don't think
so!"

"I told you, He doesn't take a hand in these
matters. These rules are irreversible, like the laws of

physics on earth. Once they're in motion, they can't be stopped. As long as I got you to admit you ran out on the fight, and I got killed because you could've prevented it, then, tag, you're *it!*"

Something was lacking in his conviction. Why hadn't he just struck me dead and taken over without all this hoopla?

"Okay, if that's how it is, I've got no problem with you taking over this old diseased body and me going to a place where I can see my family and pets and old friends. It sounds like a good trade to me."

"I don't want your body. I would have to start over…" Lenny's face melted into a look of both anticipation and regret. "The truth is that I want out of this friggin' boring place so much that I'm willing to start over again, in a womb, with no recollections of anything before that. It's some kind of math theory, where a number of deaths contribute to a ratio of births, so Earth's population doesn't go crazy. Anyway, when this opportunity with the storm came up, I jumped at it…at the chance of being born again. Somebody's going to take my place, and I don't care who it is!"

Lenny as a newborn baby. What a sight. I smiled for a split second before regaining my composure.

"You don't care who it is?" I questioned. "So, trying to con me into believing that I was the target is nothing but bullshit?"

Lenny shook a fiery index finger at me. His lips parted and stretched back, and I saw no jagged teeth. *A shark with no bite. With no bite in his threats.* "If it was in my power, you'd be dead right now, but I can't kill you, either by the rules or physically. I figured at your age and in your condition, maybe I could get you all worked up after you admitted it, and you'd have a heart attack."

"Sorry to disappoint, and what is it with using Speedo and…" I pointed at Sonny, "our buddy there?"

"The little jerk had a change of heart, but he unwittingly managed to set you up anyway, when you began to think everything in our world was honky-dory, and just as long as you didn't say something incriminating…but then Sonny took over, gave you some more of our retro visual-aids on the TV, kind of like your life passing before your eyes before the final moment. That made you even more comfortable, so he buttered you up until you spilled your little secret.

"I was pretty sure I couldn't show up alone and just bully it out of you. Those tactics didn't work when I was alive. So, there I would be with this one chance that I won't get again till who-knows-when. I needed their help in kind of seducing you, so I promised them my points—you know, like the ones Speedo told you your mother used for you—which I never used when I got there, and a lot more that I conned some poor jerks outta when they checked in. With my record, I would've needed a lot more points than I have to move on, so I bet them all on this one-shot deal. Now my man, here, gets the whole bundle, because the grease monkey didn't do nothin' to earn any. Sonny gets enough points for him to move on, and I get to return to in-body."

"Well, I'll tell you right now, you aren't coming back into this world on my soul."

Lenny's thin lips curled back into a closed-mouth, disdainful smile. "Okay, so you're not in danger, and I can't get you to croak from old age. So if I can't get who I'm after, then maybe someone else he knows is in a vulnerable situation and can be a substitute."

I smiled, not really understanding his statement. Then it hit me. "Gwen?"

"Bingo!"

"You son of a bitch."

I lunged at him. He disappeared and instantly reappeared in front of the fireplace, looking like a demon glowing in the fires of Hell.

"No." I shook my head. "You can't get her. She's safe at a rest stop. She never did anything to you. Even with your trumped-up rules, she can't be held responsible for what I did."

"Guess again." Lenny rested an outstretched transparent arm across the mantle. "When two people are together for as long as you and her, they become soul mates, joined as one in spirit. If I can't get one-half of that union, I'll get the other. What happens to the remaining half is not my concern. I've got my hooks in, the entity takes my place, and I'm back in-body."

"Hey, Lenny, you didn't say anything about getting his wife involved," Sonny said. "I didn't—"

"That's right, you didn't," Lenny spit out to Sonny. "You didn't read all the rules. I was the only one who made sure I knew every angle. So now you're just as involved as I am. No backing out."

"Who the hell wrote these rules?" I shouted. I looked over at Sonny.

He nodded, and his stone face was sympathetic to my plight but confirmed that Lenny was probably right.

"I refuse to believe this." I leaned forward and

closed my eyes. "This is bullshit." I placed my hands on my bent knees. "This is not happening." I pinched my leg again and felt the twinge of pain. My breath was shallow. "No, I'm asleep. I'm asleep."

Lenny's laugh was a low chuckle. Sonny only coughed. Then silence.

I wish them away. I wish them away. They're gone. They were never here.

I opened my eyes and found myself staring at that arrogant, thin smile on that shark face. The flames were dancing behind him and through him, and I recalled the paintings and symbolisms of Satan that we mortals conceived his image to be. No tail. No horns. But he could definitely be a model posing for Da Vinci or Michelangelo.

I stood erect. "She's safe at a rest stop. I know it for a fact. She's not out in the storm, in any danger, or vulnerable to you."

"We'll see about that," Lenny said. Then he disappeared.

I turned to Sonny.

"I'm sorry, Jimmy," he said. Then he was gone.

I was numb for a moment, trying desperately

to awake from a dream that I finally had to accept as a rude awakening of reality. Something was going to happen. Something bad.

I turned my head, and the red blinking light caught my attention. It was the answering machine. *Didn't I reset it? It's still flashing. I—Maybe it's a new message that came in unnoticed while I was involved with my tormenting specters.*

I limped to the kitchen counter, lifted the receiver, and poked the replay button.

"I don't know what's going on there," Gwen's voice said clearly, but with a definite tremor. "Why aren't you picking up the phone? I'm starting back out. I can't get through to any of our local municipalities or the state police or our neighbors to have them check on you. I have to get home to you. I love you, and I'll do my best to get there. Please…please, don't be…Don't…" She began crying. "Don't you dare!" she screamed, before the message ended with a *Whump*.

"No! No, don't *you* dare!" I screamed aloud. "Stay where you are! Stay…stay…" The phone clattered to the counter, and I lowered my head next to it, cupping my face in my hands. "I'm dreaming. Somebody tell me I'm dreaming. I can't believe…can't believe they can do what…they say…"

58

My breath came in shallow pants. I stood and gasped, again, three frightening times before catching a gulp of air. "Where's my puff…puffer?"

I turned to the sofa and saw the green plastic-cased inhaler on the end table. It was next to the extension phone—which was off its cradle. *Damn, did I leave it off the hook? Maybe they managed to take it off during our reunion without me knowing. That's why neither extension rang.*

I limped and stumbled around the near side of the couch and fell forward toward the table. My lungs felt like balloons unable to inflate; the carbon dioxide wasn't dispersing completely to allow fresh air to refill them. I scrambled into a dog walk, and the cushions sank in beneath the weight of my hands and knees. I snatched the respirator and shoved the mouthpiece between my lips in one sweeping motion. I turned and fell into a supine position, the back of my head bouncing off the upholstered sofa arm. I activated the vial and sucked in the medicated mist. Again. I wheezed as I exhaled. It wasn't working completely, not like it usually did. I activated it a third time. No, too much is no good, either. I lay quiet, trying to be calm, trying to take short breaths. My heart was pounding. My body was responding to this new danger, this gripping stress that clutched my chest. I closed my eyes and tried to make my mind a blank slate. Impossible.

59

Maybe she'll call again. Then I can warn her. I can tell her to get off the road. Wait! The phone. I stretched behind me, feeling for the handset. The back of my hand slid across the marble tabletop, and I managed to roll the receiver into the cradle with my outstretched fingers. I turned like a chicken on a spit, still in an outstretched position, until something inside me felt like it snapped, as if a rubber band somewhere in my chest sprang off its hook. I froze in place. I wheezed again. My fingers fumbled for the phone. The flickering fireplace went out. At least I think it did. Everything was black. But my eyes weren't closed. Still, everything was black. My arm relaxed. I wheezed once more. Then the blackness engulfed me.

*****

Thin bands of light ran across the carpeting just below my face. They were a sharp contrast to the rippling dark threads that bound the design together. The lighted strips were evenly spaced, framed in a neat, boxed-in pattern. My mind became more lucid, and my eyes followed the rows of luminous stripes to the front wall and the Venetian blinds covering the window. The light was flowing through the partial opening between the angled slats. It grew brighter and reflected off the blinds, lighting the room into a brilliant glow.

I took a breath and found my lungs to be flexible again. The oxygen-enhanced blood reached my brain, and I became conscious of what the light meant. I sprang instantly into a sitting position and then to my feet, like a gymnast recovering after a dismount.

She's home! It has to be her. She made it!

I was at the front door in what seemed like two leaps and swung it open with flair. The brightness that had coaxed me from the couch disappeared, as though the opening door had activated an off-switch. Whipping snow and darkness was all I saw at first beyond the frost-covered glass storm door. The porch light only illuminated the section of the deck and railing in front of the door. I rubbed the condensation from the glass to form a circular viewing area, and I could see a large, dark shape embedded in the glimmering white downfall. It was a vehicle, but its details were hard to make out behind the less-than-transparent screen of snow. Was it…? No, it was an SUV, not our Caravan. It was someone else, coming to rescue me.

The gray mass seemed to expand as both front doors swung open. They slammed shut, the sound muffled by the insulation of fallen snow, and two gray human figures appeared in their place. I pushed open the storm door, and a gust of wind planted a slap of icy flakes against the side of my face. I brushed at my wet cheek and then held my hand out to try to ward off the blowing snow.

"Man, am I glad to see you," I shouted, not caring who they were. "Come on in, please."

They trudged through the once-virgin thick white blanket to the mound that sat atop the three front steps leading to the porch. Single file, with hooded heads bowed, they ascended the hidden steps, looking like two mountain climbers. The first man raised his head as he reached the lighted porch deck, and I was happy to see a smile inside the fleece lined parka that shrouded the rest of his face.

"Can some weary travelers get a New Year's drink at this joint?" the man asked as he tugged back his hood.

I immediately recognized both the voice and the face. "Johnny! What the hell...?" My hand shot down from its outstretched position.

Johnny Wilson grasped my outstretch hand with both of his, then leaned forward and hugged me. "It wasn't this hard getting here last time we visited," he said.

"Sure, not much snow around here on the

Fourth of July," I said.

Pete Wilson immediately grasped me in a bear hug and lifted me from my feet after Johnny stepped inside. My breath rushed from my lungs, but I felt no ill effects.

"I thought I saw the Abominable Snowman leaning against your mailbox," Pete said as he let me down.

"I can't believe I'm seeing you guys." I closed the two doors after Pete was inside and flicked on the room lights. I stood and stared at my two oldest and closest friends as they removed their coats. They shook the snow from the jackets over the entry rug, stomping and wiping their feet before removing their black rubber overshoes.

They hadn't changed at all since I last saw them on that holiday weekend.

Johnny, tall and lanky, not more than ten pounds gained since we were kids, had a salt-and-pepper crew cut and had been wearing wire-rimmed glasses for about ten years.

Pete was the shortest of the Mutt and Jeff duo. He was the youngest of our trio but had aged in appearance more rapidly. His baby-fine hair was full, still in a slicked-back style, but was completely white, as were his neatly trimmed mustache and goatee. His chubby cheeks were bright crimson from the cold. The two foster brothers wore similar stylish sweaters over open-collared white shirts and dark slacks.

I motioned to the coat rack, but they knew the layout of the house and were already hanging their parkas on two unused pegs. They turned to me.

"So, where's the missus?" Johnny asked, as he rubbed his hands together to warm them.

My stomach churned as my mind replayed Gwen's message. "She's stuck out in this crap," I said. "She's out there…in danger." I explained her trip and phone messages, and then realized they had made it here with what seemed like very little effort. "How did you guys get here? And…why? What were you doing out in this?"

"Caught us by surprise, just as you said it did Gwen," Johnny said. "We have to be in Albany by tomorrow for a meeting the next day, to sign a new contract for the labor union we administer." He walked to me and grasped my shoulder. "She's gonna be fine. The Thruway isn't too bad. They have trucks out shoveling and sanding."

"Yeah, not like this dinky burg you live in," Pete said with a smile. "They oughta get some four-wheel-drive vehicles, like our Escalade. We blasted right through all this mess."

"And I'm glad you did. Damn, what time is it? I fell asleep, and…" My eyesight was a little fuzzy, but it looked like quarter after eleven on the mantle clock.

"Less than an hour before the ball drops," Johnny confirmed. "We can't stay for too long; need to get there, settle in, and prepare for the meeting—so break out the booze, my man."

"You bet."

I opened the glass breakfront of the china cabinet and lifted out bottles of Cutty Sark and Smirnoff. Johnny and Pete followed me to the kitchen area, where I retrieved glasses, ice, and mixers. They studied the photos on the refrigerator door and mumbled remarks and chuckles in reminiscence while I fixed the drinks.

We toasted the coming New Year, made some comments of pleasure after a few sips, exchanged some small talk, and then fell silent.

They were my very best friends and confidants for most of my life, tolerating—at times, seemingly encouraging—my moody, bizarre behavior as a teen. Johnny told me later in life that everyone has the right to be and to act as differently as possible to show that he or she is an individual. I knew how they thought and how they reacted to things, but I was still hesitant to tell them about my ghost story. I guessed they might try to believe me, and knowing them as I did, I'd be a good judge of any attempt to patronize me—although they very rarely did—at which point I'd drop the whole thing and make it into a joke. Here goes.

"You won't believe who visited me tonight," I said.

"What? Someone else was here before us?" Pete asked.

"In a manner," I said. "Speedo. And Sonny." No reaction. "And Lenny."

"Now I know those ain't the names of the Three Stooges or the Marx Brothers," Pete said. "But I also know that they're all just as dead."

"And they still are, but they were here, I guess you could say in spirit."

"So you're seeing ghosts?"

"Seeing, talking to, and being threatened by."

"Didn't you say you fell asleep before we got here?" Johnny asked.

"I know what you're gonna say. I was awake. I pinched myself repeatedly to be sure. I'm black and blue from all the pinching." I rolled down the waistband of my sweatpants and showed them my thigh. "Well, it should be bruised from…"

They were smiling.

"I wasn't asleep, and I wasn't dreaming," I said dejectedly as I snapped the waistband back in place. "I know what happened, and I know that Lenny is going to try to do something to Gwen. She's going to take my place for…for, uh, something I did."

Johnny placed his glass on the counter. "Jimmy, you can't think like that. Nothing is going to happen to Gwen. You know you've got that wild writer's imagination. That's what fueled it." He leaned his forearm on the counter. "Tell me what you…encountered before we got here."

"What I encountered was those three guys psychoanalyzing, schmoozing, or threatening me. Lenny wanted my soul, but when I called his bluff, he said he'd take Gwen's instead. They were here, and they were real. I couldn't make up something like this; it's too bizarre."

"That's for sure," Pete said. "Maybe you should write it down while it's fresh in your mind. Might make a good story. "

Johnny stood and poked Pete with his elbow. "Be nice." He took a sip of his drink. "You said that Lenny wanted to harm you or Gwen for something you did. What did you mean by that?"

I took a deep breath and stared them in the eyes, switching my focus between them. *I have to tell them. It's time that everyone knows, especially them.*

"Our little adventure into that psycho militant group's headquarters back around forty years ago…" I scrutinized their faces, trying to remove the vestiges of age to visualize them—and myself—as the young, healthy guys we had been back then, in the prime of our lives. "Well, when the shooting began, I…" *Say it fast.* "I ran. I took off like a scared rabbit. I left you guys behind when you needed me the most."

"So?" Johnny asked unperturbedly.

"You don't find that damning? You don't think I'm the lowest piece of crap? I know I do! I had no right being with you guys. I had no right to leave there alive, while others died."

"I'll tell you something, looking back," Pete said. "If I didn't start the whole thing, being the hothead I was, and wasn't in a position to break free, I would've been right behind you."

"You were unarmed," Johnny said, pointing at

me. "You did what any prudent person would do."

"I could've picked up one of the rifles off a dead militant. I could've done something. Not run like…I don't know, like the yellow punk Lenny accused me of being."

"Never mind about what you think Lenny thought of you. I always felt it was us that ran out on you, after you turned up missing in the shuffle, and *you know* I was relieved when you showed up later, alive and well."

"I was sure you wouldn't blame me, but I just couldn't make myself admit to what I did. You made it too easy for me to forget about it on the surface. Inside I saw myself as a coward. I tried desperately to keep myself together until the whole affair was over, but later, once it *was* in the past, I chickened out even further by putting it on the back burner and keeping it bottled up all these years."

"You came through for us many times after that shootout," Pete said. "You saved *my* bacon when I wasn't thinking straight. There's nothing to forgive, so forget you ever said anything."

I was silent, weighing the good of their exoneration against the evil of Lenny's condemnation.

"Maybe that was one of the reasons you

couldn't resolve your frustrations all these years," Johnny said. "One little guilt trip like that starts to fester, and before you know it, you start to question other actions or decisions you made through the years. Let it all go. Let go of everything that ever bothered you. You did nothing wrong."

"I sure will try now." I lifted my glass in a salute. "Thanks for your usual understanding, guys."

"But I'll bet it still felt good to get something like that off your chest, right?" Johnny asked.

I nodded. Yes, I did finally feel relieved, confident of the absolution of my sin. The more people I confessed to, the more relieved I felt. I would tell Gwen as soon as I saw her.

"So, getting back to what started this, you said that Lenny was going to do something to you or Gwen for that little incident?"

"Yeah. He says he has the…I guess you'd call it the right of law where they are, to replace me or Gwen for what I did to him; for getting him killed by my actions." I glanced at the phone. "She's still out there." I took a quick swallow of my vodka and seven. "He can still get her."

"You can't believe everything you hear from a ghost," Pete said. He reached out and slapped my arm, his genuine smile showing me he was only trying to relieve my tension. "You know what my mom used to say? It isn't the dead you have to fear, but the living."

"You know what happened?" Johnny said. "You had those three guys on your mind—maybe you were reminiscing, being here alone—and you fell asleep and created this scenario because you still felt guilty. You knew Lenny was a badass. He was always trying to bully somebody, and that's how he came across in your dream. You were punishing yourself for what you thought you did wrong by having him threaten you with taking away your life or by taking away one of the most precious things in your life."

"But it was too real."

"Sure. Because it was very vivid in your mind." Johnny pointed at me. "Let me tell you something about Lenny and most of the tough guys we knew. They had an inferiority complex. At least you wore yours on your sleeve. You had the courage to show your inner self and sometimes be held up to ridicule for it." He dropped his hand to his drink. "They were the ones that ran. They ran from their inner selves all their lives and hid behind their rough-and-tumble front. Sure, they were physically tough and intimidating, but inside they were no different from you. That's why Lenny barely scared you in life.

You unconsciously knew what he really was. Don't let him scare you in death. Fight him. He's no different from those condescending jocks who prompted you to join the Vandals to be free of their scorn. They all wanted to feel superior, and the only way was to try to extort some form of power over you."

"But you thought I was dream—"

"Fight him in your mind," Johnny interrupted. He took a swallow of his scotch. "That's where he is, in your mind. Tell him you now have the power, the power of your mind over his and all those from your past. Let them take their petty little one-track minds and get the hell out of your head, because you have the greater mind, a mind that can reach out to many facets, rather than just what their limited vision can see."

Pete applauded. "I hope you can be as impressive when you address the arbitrators day after tomorrow."

"I'll knock 'em dead," Johnny said with a wink. He drained the last of his scotch, and then slid the glass into the center of the counter. "That's what I was meant to do. We all have a purpose in life. The purpose of the four guys who didn't survive that escapade was to give their lives for its success. The purpose of the four who made it is only partially evident."

"What about Red?" I asked, remembering the fourth survivor. "He was killed in Viet Nam on his third tour." I suddenly realized that Speedo had never mentioned seeing Red.

"And he died a hero. The Silver Star, just missing out on the Medal of Honor posthumously," Johnny said. "His purpose was to keep his platoon from being wiped out. That's why he was spared, so he could eventually save those men."

That's why he wasn't trapped in that limbo plane with Speedo and the others. He went straight through the tunnel into the light for what he did.

"That leaves us three," Johnny said. "We will all know our ultimate single purpose in due time."

"But my immediate purpose is to keep Gwen safe," I said. "If I could only face up to Lenny again, I'd gladly trade myself for Gwen. I'll let them do what they want to me. I'll do it to myself, if…"

"Stop talking nonsense. You *can* keep her safe," Johnny said. "You don't have to face anyone, and you don't have to sacrifice yourself. You just have to know she's safe, and nothing will harm her. That's all there is to it. Faith. I guarantee she'll make it home soon. All you have to do is set your mind to it."

Easier said than done. I did feel more relaxed from Johnny's encouragement, but I wasn't thoroughly convinced I had been dreaming. I was still scared.

"Okay, I'll tell you what," Johnny said, either seeing or feeling my reluctance. "We're gonna leave in a minute or so…"

"Ah, come on, have one more drink," I urged. I glanced at the microwave clock as I lifted the bottle of Cutty Sark. "It's still another fifteen minutes until midnight."

"No," Johnny said, waving off the bottle. "I'm gonna do the driving on our last leg. As I started to say, what we could do for you is to search for Gwen. We have to go back to the Thruway to continue north. Instead, we'll head south until the next rest stop. We'll keep a sharp eye out for your van on the road, and if we see her, we'll turn around at the next opportunity, catch up to her, because I'm sure she'll be driving slowly, and we'll follow her home. If not, when we get to the rest stop, if she's there we'll bring her home in our SUV. You can get a ride back to pick up the van when the weather clears."

"But you have a schedule to keep," I said.

"We don't have anything pressing to do when we get there. We'll have plenty of time before the meeting. This is more important."

"Damn, I wish I could do something to repay you. I wanna go with you."

"No, you stay by the phone in case she calls. Then you can tell her to watch for us."

"But..."

"Here's something you can do for me," Pete said, sliding his empty glass in front of me. "I'm not driving."

"It's settled," Johnny said. "When we bring her home, we can all celebrate the new year together. I have to use your little boys' room, then we'll be on our way."

I started to point toward the bathroom, but Johnny was already at the hall. I poured only a splash of scotch, at Pete's direction, over the half-melted ice and diluted residue in his glass.

"We're gonna be absolutely committed that she gets home safe," Pete said before lifting the glass and downing the scotch and soda. "You can make book on it."

"No, that's one of your rackets," I said with a smile. "Wouldn't want to muscle in on you guys. I'm glad, though, to know you only handle bookmaking, loans and union sweetheart deals."

"That's what kept us out of jail. This area up here in God's country is ready for some new blood," Pete said. "You're welcome to help us branch out."

"You know Johnny wouldn't let me get involved in any of your…enterprises. He wanted me to stay clean." I took a sip of my drink. "I'm glad he did. Not only am I too old to get into something like that, but I'm happy with what I've got, and I'm comfortable with my status quo."

"I know. I was just joshin'. You stay on the track you're on, and hopefully soon…well, you'll find that ultimate purpose Johnny said we all had."

"Talking about me?" Johnny asked as he emerged from the hall.

"Of course," Pete said. "Who's always at the center of all our conversations?" He pushed off the counter. "Come on, let's get searching so we can get this gentleman and his lady reunited."

"Please," I said, my head bowed. "Give me one minute." I raised my head and my glass. "There has never been a night in my life like this one. It's not often that someone opens his eyes, heart, and mind at the same time. I will never again blame others for my self-imposed problems—actually, I will never again harbor any self-imposed problems—and I'll always remember that there is nothing like family and friends, especially when there is no difference between the two. Should old acquaintance—never—be forgot in days of auld lang syne. To my friends who are my family." I downed the remainder of my vodka to keep my dry throat from closing up from emotion.

Neither of them had a drink, but they looked at me with that warm glow of recognition, like what I would've liked my father to have bestowed upon me over one of my accomplishments, or maybe even one of the jocks, if I had made a spectacular catch in the outfield. It was never too late to merit such a look, and I accepted it as the culmination of recognition I deserved in the past, all rolled into one ingenuous expression—sort of like a lifetime achievement award.

"Thanks again, guys," I said as I followed them to the coat rack. "You're welcome to stay here the night and start out early tomorrow. Anything you want to do, I'm here for you."

"First, we're here for you," Pete said as he slid into his parka.

"We'll figure everything out as soon as we get back here with Gwen," Johnny said with a grunt, as he pulled on his rubber overshoes.

We didn't say good-bye. I was confident of their return as I watched them file through the doorway into the bluster and cold of the night. They had never let me down before, and I had no reason to believe they wouldn't come through for me now.

I snapped on the spotlights to help them navigate their descent down the now-larger mound that covered the steps. Their strides thrust the static snow along their route into the air. It mixed with falling flakes and blended into crystal clouds that sparkled in the glow of the spotlights. The impressions of their previous path had disappeared, filled in by the wind-borne snowfall.

"Be careful," I shouted into the wind as the Escalade doors slammed shut. "Make sure you all get back here safe."

The engine's ignition roared, and then its sound diminished to an almost inaudible hum, muffled by the built-up covering of snow on the hood. In less than a minute, the gray shape merged with and then vanished into the white backdrop. Another minute, and the sound of the tires crunching into snow disappeared.

I left the spotlights on as a directional beacon for their return. I closed the doors and snapped off the interior light, returning my surroundings to the earlier atmosphere of the night. I sat on the couch next to the phone and looked at the white, dormant screen of the television set. The damn thing had been on all along, without sound or picture, just waiting for my return.

Alone again. Everything seemed to be as it was before all my visitors. Except...I looked at the mantle clock. About two more minutes. The remote sat next to the phone. I lifted it and pressed the channel button. Times Square and its tumultuous throng filled the screen. It was present-day Times Square. No trips back to my past this time. The four numerals of what would be the New Year were waiting, outlined in hundreds of darkened light bulbs below the vertical track that the shining ball would descend upon. There was only a trace of snow falling. The storm must have stayed north of the city.

God, but Dick Clark looked so emaciated and frail. He could barely talk. *Why is he still hosting this event?* I remembered *American Bandstand*, when he was young and vibrant and his audiences even more so. He was part of our past, no flashbacks needed, no tricky recreations by the ghost world. He was right there in front of me, and he was a representative of what was left of the influential voices of my generation. The old trying to grasp for its last hurrah, all of us wanting that last chance to have a spotlight shine on us in glory—either again or for the first time—before it's all over. *If Johnny is right about a person's place in destiny, then what is it that I'm*

79

destined for—and will I have to prove myself to an   `
audience or only to myself?

The ball was starting to move, slowly shimmying along its support, heading for that point of renewal, of a new year and new resolutions to transform what had been wrong with the past. If only we could keep those resolutions. If only they didn't gradually deteriorate, slowly fading from the enthusiasm of professing to the promise of change, leaving the same life and same behavior, and usually the same disappointments, before suddenly resurrected on the following year's final day of December.

This was life. Only a few kept their resolutions—not the declarations of losing weight or stopping smoking, but the true life changes, mind-altering decisions. The spotlight was for those who knew there were things wrong and who had the courage to change them. Sometimes the spotlight was from the public domain, but mostly it was from themselves or their closest confidants, those who really benefited from that New Year's resolution.

I had made a start; now I must continue with that resolution to never again keep things to myself or blame anyone but myself for the problems I create. It was too late in my life to keep secrets, secrets that corrupted the mind. Gwen—who should've been the first—would be the next to know about everything that ever bothered me. I was very confident that she would be even more understanding than Johnny and Pete. I owed thanks not only to Johnny and Pete but also to the trio who thought they were conning me. If not for their intervention, I'd still be wallowing around in my self-pity.

They had been my friends, and, knowingly or not, they acted as such. Inadvertently or not, they had given me the strength to carry on and admit my inner faults. They, with their desperate schemes and final capitulation to my stubbornness, had started me on this road of discovery and renewal. Now that I had convinced myself that Gwen would return to me safe, I had no animosity toward any of them. For a brief moment, I considered their visit a practical joke or elaborate plan with the ultimate intention of producing this exact outcome. *Thank you, my Vandal comrades, whatever your intentions.*

The ball touched the top of the numerals and they lit. The roar of thousands of voices soared from the television speakers and drowned out Dick Clark's slurred, feeble words. His courage to go on motivated me, as he tried to speak in the face of an overwhelming din, and I then knew why he did what he did. We all had to constantly prove ourselves, no matter what the opposition, through our vulnerabilities and challenges—physical, emotional, or mental—and keep that sense of dignity that others might be trying to take from us. With age comes wisdom. Some of us—yes, like me—don't realize that wisdom until late in life. Maybe it wasn't too late.

The screen was getting fuzzy, and I wondered if I was about to be treated to another nostalgic trip. A warm numbness and lightheadedness crept over my body. I wished that Gwen were with me. It was the first New Year's Eve in over four decades that she wasn't by my side. The images on the television were blurred outlines, and I was surprised that a beer and a vodka had affected me this much. *I have to…stay awake…* The television and all of the furniture looked like they were made of clay, twisting and reshaping into weird forms. *By the phone in case…* Someone other than Dick Clark was speaking, the voice off in a distant tunnel. I fell asleep.

*****

My mouth was extremely dry. I was breathing okay, but it didn't feel natural. There was something in my nostrils, and I could feel a flow of fresh air in my nasal passages. I was on my back, and there was softness beneath me, but a different softness than our couch. My ankle hurt and I remembered twisting it earlier. There were other pains and stiffness in my shoulders and neck. I opened my eyes to a blurred vision of strange surroundings, somewhere that I was sure wasn't my home. The walls were green. My focus sharpened. There was an overhead railing, and a curtain hanging from it. It was a circular railing around…I was in a bed. There were tubes and wires flowing along my partially bare chest like tiny pipelines along a stubbly hilltop.

"He's awake," a female voice said.

She was dressed in white. A nurse. She moved aside, and Gwen was standing there. *Thank goodness. Gwen is okay.*

"He'll get acclimated soon," the nurse's voice said. She moved to another part of the room, and I wasn't sure, but I may have drifted off to sleep again.

"Gwen. Where am I?" I asked when I opened my eyes.

""You're okay, honey." Her words were tender. "They got to you in time."

"In time? I'm in a hospital?"

"Yes."

"He looks like he's breathing fine," the nurse said, stepping back into my view at the foot of the bed. She leaned down, and I heard a cranking sound. The upper section of the bed slowly rose to allow me to sit upright. "I'll leave you two to chat. If you need me, I'll be just next door at the nurse's station."

"Thank you." Gwen watched the nurse leave, and then turned back to me.

I watched her silently smooth out the side of my blanket and then sit on the edge of the bed. I raised my hand to touch her arm and saw the plastic bracelet on my wrist. "Can I have a drink of water?" I asked.

Gwen partially filled a glass from a pitcher she lifted off my bedside table. She held the glass with a straw for me to sip. When my mouth felt refreshed, I released the straw, and she placed the glass back onto the table. She turned back to me, a photo in her hand.

"They found this in your sweatpants pocket," she said. "You must have been looking at it right before you…" She silently handed me the refrigerator door photo.

I wasn't completely coherent, but some details looked different from the first time I had seen it. I dropped it back on the table.

"What happened?" I asked. "Right before I

what?"

She bent down and kissed me, stroked my hair back from my forehead and smiled. She was silent, and I wasn't sure if I was still in a groggy state of mind and not comprehending an answer, or if she was deliberately not answering. I studied her for a moment. Her narrow, almost wrinkle-free face didn't show her true age; pale blue eyes were emphasized by silver, medium-length hair, with strands of her original ash blond still weaving through and giving off an almost metallic sheen. She wore only a hint of makeup and still possessed the beauty and poise of her earlier career as a dancer.

"I had finally gotten through to our local volunteer ambulance service on my cell phone. The paramedics saved your life," she finally said, with the whisper of a sob in her voice. "When they found you, you had stopped breathing. They revived you and rushed you here. Thank God, the doctors found no permanent damage."

"How'd they get to me? Did you and Johnny and Pete find me passed out?"

"Johnny and Pete?" She seemed startled. "Honey, I'm sorry…I don't know why you thought of them, but…they're dead. They were killed in a car accident."

I think I groaned. The once monotonous, steady bleep of a nearby machine suddenly accelerated, along with my heartbeat.

"Take it easy, honey. I shouldn't have told you." She stroked my hair again. "Don't think about it. You'll only make things worse."

I tried to ignore what Gwen had told me, as if she had never said it, as if I only imagined her saying it. *It just can't be! They were supposed to come back. We were all supposed to celebrate. They were part of my family. They were like my brothers. No! Oh, God, no! I loved those guys. I know they felt the same about me, and it had to be them that had a hand in saving me. Now I have to calm down, or what they did will be in vain. Calm down. Relax.*

"Is everything okay?" the nurse asked from the doorway. "His EKG monitor in my station took a spike, and—"

"I'm fine," I said. I shook off the initial grief and heard the machine bleeps slow to a normal pace. "I was just happy to be reunited with my wife, if you know what I mean."

The nurse laughed, then joked, "Please try to control yourself, sir." She stepped away, probably returning to her station.

I closed my eyes for a moment. "You know they got killed for us," I said. "They insisted on looking for you, to get you home safely."

"I don't understand," Gwen said. "How could you have thought something like that?"

"Because they were at our house." I opened my eyes. "They left me home to stay by the phone while they went out into the storm for you. I guess they never found you."

"Something doesn't make sense here." Gwen leaned in closer to me, placing her hand next to my head for support. "They couldn't have been at our house. An eighteen-wheeler hit their SUV near Yonkers. They were killed instantly, nowhere near our town."

I suppose I looked like the village idiot with my jaw hanging down on my chest. *This can't be. I know what I saw.* "Wait…When were they killed?"

"The newscasts say earlier in the evening, between six and seven. I probably passed the same spot where it happencd less than a half-hour later."

"My God, they took our place."

"What?"

"They replaced you and me to satisfy Lenny.

Two people so close that they are one in spirit. That was them. They were always together. They were closer than real brothers, even though they were only foster brothers. I saw them; I touched them, and they were solid flesh and bone. Not like the others."

Gwen now emulated my drop-jaw expression.

Okay, let's start this new era of honesty and openness, even if it makes you sound like a lunatic. I told her everything about my evening, from the appearance of Speedo to Johnny and Pete leaving our driveway.

"You have to know that you were dreaming," she said, sitting up. "You were alone…looking for company in your mind. These things happen."

"You forgot about my writer's imagination. All of them—including me—threw that in." A few facts and calculations began to come together in my mind. "I just thought of something. You say that the paramedics said I had stopped breathing?"

Gwen nodded.

"So I was clinically dead for some short period of time, a minute or so. Then I must have been on the same plane as them. That's why I could touch them, why my breathing was normal, why my twisted ankle and old age pains weren't evident. Like a dream that seems like hours only takes a few seconds to run through your mind, so it was with my visit from Johnny and Pete. They already knew they were taking our places and they wanted to keep me from doing something stupid, and to assure me that you would return home safe."

"There's something strange I didn't tell you," Gwen said, her expression now sympathetic to my tale. "When I reached the ambulance station, I wasn't dialing them. I didn't know their direct number. I was calling home, trying to reach you, but the call went to their station. The dispatcher was surprised that I got through to them because a lot of phone lines were down, and so was their ambulance radio from the unusual weather conditions. We assumed it was crossed lines or momentary atmospheric clearance that rang me through to them. He said they had felt helpless without any way for people to reach them, and a crew was about to start out on a patrol of the main streets. A minute or so later, and I would've missed them. He had them head right out to check on you."

"It was Johnny and Pete. They directed your call there. It had to be."

She looked down and nodded. "Something happened," she agreed. "Someone—a lot of us, real and in spirit, wanted you to live."

"It was them," I repeated. "First my mother, and now them. I owe so many of my loved ones for my continued life. I must still fit into some grand plan that I have to stick around for."

"We're all part of a grand plan. Maybe we've already accomplished our part by having Matt and Karen, and Karen, in turn, having Paul and Timmy to continue our bloodline, and one of them is destined to do something great or beneficial for humanity. Our part in it was to have them and nurture them."

"Maybe that's part of it, but all those sacrifices weren't made if there wasn't something more ahead. I lived a lot of my life in my fantasies and dreams, escaping there to occasionally avoid the reality of my life, my fears and my disappointments, but now it's time to live all of my life in reality. I'm sure I wasn't dreaming, but what I experienced was definitely a wakeup call. Wake up and live. There isn't much more time to do it in." I fell silent, reflecting on what I had just said. "Maybe it's borrowed time," I mumbled.

"Whatever it is, we'll find out together." Gwen clutched my hand. "That's my last trip and my last New Year's Eve without you next to me."

"Amen."

We quietly pondered our fate, until Gwen

broke the silence. "I wasn't allowed in here while they were prepping you with your breathing tubes and paraphernalia, so I took a stroll down to the maternity ward to look at the new babies. They happened to be on display then." She smiled and stared off into the distance. "They're so tiny and fragile. It was nice to see a newborn again. It's been such a long time since our last grandchild was born.

"Most newborns are wrinkly and not very beautiful, but there was this one that was very unusual, to say the least. In addition to him being premature and underweight, his face was kind of shaped like a cone and came to a point at his nose."

"Oh, no. It can't be. Not so soon." I tightened my grip on Gwen's hand. "You never met Crazy Lenny, did you?"

"The guy you said you dreamed…or I mean, you saw as a ghost? No, I never had the pleasure." She smiled. "Why?"

"You just described what he would look like as a baby."

"Honey, this can't be. It's just a coincidence."

"No, look…" I stretched to the bedside table, retrieved the photo and starred at it. *I was right, it was different.* The grouping had changed. I'm off alone at

the far right edge. Lenny is alone at the far left edge.
Bunched together in the center are the other four.
"Take a look at this guy on the left." I held the picture
out for Gwen to scrutinize.

"You mean Johnny? He's the furthest to the
left."

I yanked the picture back into my view. *What
the hell!* Lenny was gone. There were only five of us
in the picture. I dropped the hand holding the picture
onto my leg and closed my eyes. Somebody out there
was still playing games with my head.

"How are you two doing?" the nurse asked
from the direction of the doorway.

"Fine," Gwen said. "Right, honey?"

I opened my eyes. "Yeah, I guess as well as
can be expected."

"Remember what we were discussing earlier?"
the nurse asked Gwen.

"Yes."

The nurse beckoned Gwen with her finger to
come to her. "Excuse us a moment," the nurse said to
me.

Gwen walked to the doorway, and the two

women chatted in whispers, Gwen raising her voice slightly to utter, "Oh, no, that's a shame."

Gwen returned to my bedside and the nurse again disappeared.

"That's so sad," Gwen said as she sat back on the edge of the bed. "The nurse and I had spoken after I returned from the maternity ward, while I was waiting to see you. We talked about grandchildren and babies in general and then about that little baby with the pointy face. She called me over to tell me in secret what had happened, because she knew he intrigued me. She didn't want you to hear any kind of sad or disturbing news in your state, but I think you're up to it, and since you feel involved with him, I'll tell you. The poor thing passed away. He was too premature, too weak to make it."

I looked at the photo again. *That's why Lenny was gone. He didn't make it.* He's on his way back to limbo. Or worse. This photo was Speedo's creation. Now he's using it to tell me what's going on.

"He lost his bid to be in-body because he rushed things," I said. "He was in too much of a hurry to wait for a healthier body; it's his punishment for being a manipulator and trying to take innocent lives. If his next destination is back in limbo, he'll probably now have an even longer stay and won't have any points in his bank. Yes, I think that would be a worse

93

punishment for him than the alternative."

"Go ahead, honey," Gwen said. "Imagine for a while, but make sure you remember your pledge to return to reality."

"No, this is reality. Those four guys are all together. Sonny, who I'm sure wasn't doing what he did to hurt me but was influenced into helping a friend, must have shared Lenny's points with Speedo. There may have been enough points for the both of them to move on. Johnny and Pete either went straight to the light or were awarded enough bonus points to get them there soon, because what greater sacrifice can one make but to give their life—or in their case, their temporary place in eternity—for a friend?" I looked at the photo again. "They're standing there together, waiting for me, off by myself. They're waiting for me to join them someday."

"Not for a while," Gwen said, as she leaned in and hugged me. "Not for a while."

"No, I still have that purpose to accomplish. Every single one of us, no matter what body we're born into, is here for a reason. One of the mysteries of life. What is that reason? What is that purpose? We'll all find out someday."

End

Made in the USA
Lexington, KY
21 July 2013